Good News for All Nations

Other books by Martin Goldsmith:

God on the Move (O. M. Paternoster, 1998)
Islam and Christian Witness (O. M. Paternoster, 1982)
Jesus and His Relationships (Paternoster, 2000)
Life's Tapestry – Reflections and Insights from My Life
(O. M. Paternoster, 1997)
Matthew and Mission – the Gospel through Jewish Eyes
(Paternoster, 2001)
Serving God Today (O. M. Paternoster, 2000)
What About Other Faiths? (Hodder & Stoughton, 1989)
Who is My Neighbour? (O. M. Paternoster, 2002)

Good News
for All Nations

Mission at the Heart
of the New Testament

Martin Goldsmith

Hodder & Stoughton
LONDON SYDNEY AUCKLAND

Copyright © 2002 by Martin Goldsmith

First published in Great Britain in 2002

The right of Martin Goldsmith to be identified as the Author
of the Work has been asserted by him in accordance
with the Copyright, Designs and Patents Act 1988.

10 9 8 7 6 5 4 3 2 1

British Library Cataloguing in Publication Data
A record for this book is available from the British Library

ISBN 0 340 78609 4

Typeset by Avon Dataset Ltd, Bidford-on-Avon, Warks

Printed and bound in Great Britain by
Clays Ltd, St Ives plc

Hodder & Stoughton
A Division of Hodder Headline Ltd
338 Euston Road
London NW1 3BH
www.madaboutbooks.com

Contents

Preface   vii
Introduction   1

1   Matthew and mission: encouraging a minority   11
    Church
2   Matthew and mission: universality   30
3   Luke and the Gentiles   46
4   The gospel spreads (Acts of the Apostles)   62
5   John's Gospel: 'By believing you may have life'   84
6   Romans – Paul, apostle to the Gentiles: 112
    chapters 1 to 8
7   Romans – Paul, apostle to the Gentiles: 135
    chapters 9 to 16
8   Conclusion: 2,000 years from the New Testament   159
    to today

    Suggested reading   164

Preface

As a boy I lived for a while with my grandparents in Didsbury, south of Manchester. In those days this was a largely Jewish area and the name 'Didsbury' was commonly corrupted to become 'Yidsbury'. Likewise the main road near our home was called Palatine Road, and this too was easily adapted by adding an 's' to make it 'Palestine Road'. Our very secularised Jewish community predominated in the district around Palestine Road in West Yidsbury.

In those days neither I nor others in my family could have imagined that many years later I would be invited by a Christian college nearby to be the speaker at their annual convention. But it was a real pleasure and privilege to be asked to give the Didsbury Lectures at the Nazarene College just a few streets away from where I had lived as a boy. In a large marquee in their garden, with typical Manchester rain splattering on the roof, I gave five talks which now form the basis for the first five chapters of this book. I am deeply grateful to the leaders of the Nazarene College for inviting me and for those present who encouraged me to think of adapting the lectures for a book. It should, however, be emphasised that the content has been considerably altered since the lectures were given.

In addition to the topics which form the basis for this book, I gave one further lecture on pluralism and the Christian attitude to other faiths. In various forms, this has been the topic of numerous seminars and lectures in all sorts of churches up and down Britain as well as overseas. University students in Christian Unions have also been subjected to talks on this subject. I have discovered that it is a hot-potato topic in societies where New Age, existentialism or post-modernism influence people's thinking. Because of my book *What About Other Faiths?* (Hodder & Stoughton, 1989) I am frequently asked to address this subject. Again and again church or Christian Union leaders warn me apologetically that probably not many people will attend such a seminar. And again and again they are astonished to see how many people turn up. It is such a vitally relevant issue in our time. But in this book I will concentrate on the essential topic of the first lectures, which were on a biblical foundation for mission.

Nazarene College should in no way be held responsible for the contents of this book. If stoning is merited, all attacks should be directed at the author alone. On the other hand I wish to record my gratitude to them, as also to all the churches, colleges, Christian Unions and varied Christian conferences and institutions which graciously invite me to share my feeble insights with them. May God use even the contents of this little book as seed-thoughts to encourage others in their life and ministry in the task of Christian mission.

For twenty-four years my wife Elizabeth and I richly benefited from the enormous privilege of working as lecturers and tutors at All Nations Christian College. And still today the college very generously calls us 'associate lecturers' and invites us to play a small part in teaching there. This forms a lovely interlude in the midst of a full-time travelling ministry. It is always a special pleasure to return to All Nations, where we feel so much at home after so many years on the staff there.

While serving as a lecturer at All Nations I taught a wide variety of subjects related to Christian mission and to other faiths. One subject which always excited me was 'A Biblical Basis of Mission'. My reading, thinking, lecturing and preaching on this important topic over so many years also lay behind the talks given in Didsbury – and will also determine the contents of this book.

I want therefore to thank all the multitudes of past students at All Nations who have sat through my lectures. Many have allowed their thinking and the whole direction of their ministry to be to some extent influenced. It is such a privilege to play some small part in shaping the future ministries of those who take up the baton of mission and carry it into the future and into so many areas of the world where one cannot go oneself. I would like to dedicate this small book, therefore, to all who have paid attention in my lectures and not gone to sleep!

* For a more extensive study of Matthew and mission see M. Goldsmith, *Matthew and Mission – the Gospel through Jewish Eyes* (Paternoster, 2001).

Introduction

A large well-known evangelical church in southern England was holding a special missionary week. I was invited to be the missionary speaker on the Sunday and was staying in the comfortable and friendly home of the church's missions secretary. They were a delightful and spiritually minded couple, so it was a particular pleasure to be in their home. Their two excellently behaved young children sparkled with fun, so we could relax between meetings with a romp or a game.

Before Sunday morning breakfast my host read the story of the Good Samaritan from the New Testament and then a comment on it from some devotional Bible reading notes.

'The parable of the Good Samaritan is telling us to help people who are in need,' he explained to us as a family around the breakfast table. 'If we see a blind person wanting to cross the road or an old person who can no longer keep their kitchen clean and in order, we should be willing to give them a helping hand.'

'How true,' I thought to myself, 'but is that really the significance of this revolutionary parable?' The Old Testament abounds with exhortations to help the needy and the poor, the oppressed and the outcasts of society. And rabbinic teaching likewise overflows with this call to serve the poor. If Jesus was merely adding another story to underline all that the Old Testament and rabbinics so repeatedly taught, then the parable of the Good Samaritan was just bringing coals to Newcastle – or oranges to Tel Aviv. It would have nothing of striking interest to say.

But actually this was a radical story. Jesus shows that it was a Samaritan who helped the Jewish man in trouble. He contrasts the spirit of the Samaritan with that of the Jewish leaders. The story would have been sufficiently controversial if it had told of a Samaritan being helped by a Jewish leader. It would have been inflammatory in Jewish ears to suggest that they as Jews might have to be dependent on a despised Samaritan for help. The parable became even more objectionable in implying that a Samaritan might reflect the characteristics of the kingdom of God more than the Jewish leadership.

Yes, the parable of the Good Samaritan could have been an ideal reading in the context of that breakfast with the missionary speaker in the home of the church missions secretary during the missions weekend. The parable's emphasis on the wider purposes of God for his kingdom fitted the situation exactly. As is true of the whole of the New Testament, so also this parable emphasises that the gospel and the saving ministry of Jesus are not just for the Jews, but also for other peoples. The universality of God's kingdom stands central to the message of the New Testament. As we proceeded to our boiled eggs I reflected on the inadequate understanding of Scripture which sadly afflicts our churches. Even my host failed to see the significance of the Good Samaritan, although he was a well-taught and highly intelligent leader in a church which is known for its quality Bible teaching.

There is a danger that the exposition of God's word in our colleges and churches fails to relate to worldwide international mission. And likewise teaching on mission is often pragmatic, with stories of the work of evangelism, church ministries and social or developmental work, but these have little biblical basis. In our churches the normal biblical sermon and worship contents will have little to say about worldwide mission. And the missionary talk may start piously with a Bible verse or two, but will then move rapidly on to the actual task of mission.

As Christians, we affirm that our faith and practice are based on the Bible as our ultimate authority. If worldwide international mission is peripheral to the biblical revelation, then it should not be vitally important in the life of the Church. And those of us who are serving in the area of cross-cultural mission should appreciate that our work is not of great importance and we have no right to ask other Christians to get involved with us in prayer, giving or sacrificial service. But it is the thesis of this book that cross-cultural inter-ethnic mission worldwide is central to the message of the Bible and is therefore essential in the life of every Christian and every church.

The danger of forming a dichotomy between our biblical understanding and the practice of international mission was further underlined to me by a conversation with the new Professor of Missions in a large theological seminary in North America. He confided to me that he had radically altered the missions courses. In the past, he said, they had majored on biblical and theological understanding, but they had been unpractical and irrelevant. So now he boasted that he had scrapped all emphasis on the Bible and theology in favour of the pragmatic, the cultural and the sociological! Surely these two emphases need to be held together, recognising that the foundation of our life and faith is always the Bible.

As teachers and practitioners in the field of Christian mission worldwide, we face the challenge to be holistic. Our biblical and theological understanding needs to relate to the practical, the pastoral and every other area of life. We dare not continue a radical separation between the biblical, the theological, the historical, the pastoral and the practical. Every aspect of our Christian life and practice must be founded on a sound biblical and theological foundation which works through to the pragmatic practice of mission.

The heart of the New Testament burns with inter-ethnic and international mission. The good news of salvation in Jesus Christ is for all peoples everywhere. God loves not only Israel, but also all the world and all nations. An insular approach to Scripture reflects a misunderstanding of the very heart of God, the purposes of Jesus Christ and the mind of the Holy Spirit.

In this little book I shall restrict myself to just a few of the main New Testament writers and their books, realising of course that the other books of the New Testament were also written in the heat of their missionary situation. Likewise I shall not review the Old Testament approach to mission, although the New Testament is clearly built on the foundation of the Hebrew Scriptures. Already in the first chapters of the Bible the story of creation reveals that God is supreme over *all* people, for he created them all. Therefore the perfect image and likeness of God characterises *all* people and peoples everywhere. Then the Fall brings sin and depravity, not only to Adam and Eve, but through them to *all* humanity. Paul builds on this truth particularly in Romans.

As sin evolved and spread viciously after Adam, God called Abraham to be not only the father of Israel, but also the father of many nations. The pattern of Abraham's justification by faith continued through the history of Israel into the life of the international Church of Jesus Christ. And Israel never fully lost sight of the hope that the light of God would shine through her to *all* nations. God's wider purposes and Israel's call to be a blessing to the nations form the background to God's mission statement in the New Testament.

While lecturing at All Nations Christian College I was much impressed by *The Biblical Foundations for Mission* by D. Senior and C. Stuhlmueller (SCM, 1983), with its exposition of a missiological understanding of the Bible. Many other books on the study of mission (e.g. J. Verkuyl, *Contemporary Missiology*, Eerdmans, 1978; D. Bosch, *Transforming Mission: Paradigm Shifts in the Theology of Mission*, Orbis, 1991) may be excellent in many respects, but lack an in-depth study of the Scriptures from a missiological perspective. At All Nations we often asked students to read sections of *The Biblical Foundations for Mission* to stimulate and inspire them in their studies. Sadly, however, this book is based on a somewhat liberal view of the Bible and theology, and as a college lecturer I often longed for a more evangelical work which would combine careful academic study with a high view of the Bible as God's revealed word. More recently this need has been partly met by A. Kostenberger and P. O'Brien in their very helpful *Salvation to the Ends of the Earth* (Apollos, 2001). It is my prayer that my book may also further inspire other, better-qualified scholars to continue biblical study and teaching along this line.

The paucity of such books and of good biblical commentaries which have a missiological foundation causes real problems in our theological colleges and Bible schools. This weakness, in its turn, determines the content of preaching and teaching in our churches, as well as the content of Bible-reading notes, devotional Christian books and other literature. Thus international mission becomes an optional extra in Christian discipleship rather than an absolute essential.

Even at All Nations, with its central emphasis on cross-cultural mission, students inevitably use the accepted commentaries in their biblical studies. However much we as lecturers emphasise the missiological significance of the text, students again and again write assignments which reflect the typical non-missiological perspective of North Atlantic Gentile biblical study and theology.

Two key issues in the New Testament

Encouraging a minority Church
'Are we the only soldiers in step? Might it be possible that as Christians we have got it all wrong and the anti-Christian majority are right in their rejection of Jesus as the Messiah and Saviour?'

Inevitably the first disciples of Jesus and his other followers asked such questions. Likewise, the early Church, for whom the whole New Testament was written, must have faced similar challenges. They represented just a tiny minority among the masses of their own people. They also stemmed largely from the less-educated classes of society and so were surrounded not only by the unbelieving masses but also by a hostile elite in education, politics and religion. The first Christians were, of course, almost all Jews. But the great majority of the scribes, Pharisees and other leaders of Israel were implacably opposed to their faith in Jesus as the long-awaited Messiah. And these enemies of the Christian faith were well versed in the Bible and in its apparent prophecies concerning the coming Messiah and the messianic age. Could all these leaders be wrong? Was it just pig-headedly arrogant of the first Christians to believe in Jesus and follow him? Such doubts were exacerbated by the fierce persecution which assailed those first disciples of Jesus and the early Church.

Recently, a British Christian couple came to talk with me. 'We have been facing very real problems in our lives and in our family. The children have been ill, we've had to move house twice and we're at the end of our tether.' They went on to say how they were asking serious questions about the Christian faith and their own position as Christians. What is Jesus Christ for? What did he come for and what does he offer his people? What is the purpose of being a Christian? What do we expect in life if we belong to Jesus?

This couple were in theory strongly opposed to a theology of prosperity, but actually were deeply influenced by the assumption that as Christians we can expect the Lord to grant us all we desire in life. They had no theology of suffering except the confidence that the Holy Spirit would surely deliver them from their troubles. They were very excited when I pointed out to them that it is in suffering that we enjoy fellowship with the suffering Christ (Phil. 3:10) and that suffering can produce endurance, character and hope (Rom. 5:3, 4). Indeed, I assured them that the power, might and glory of the Lord are given to us in order that we might be able to endure suffering with that miraculous combination of patient endurance and joyful thanksgiving to our gracious Father (Col. 1:11, 12).

The early Church was evidently struggling too with such issues. Was Jesus really in charge as the Lord of history when the Christians' persecutors seemed to have all power and good repute?

The New Testament writers are therefore carefully showing that Jesus is indeed the Messiah who fulfils all the Old Testament messianic prophecies. He is indeed the true Lord and Saviour of humankind. Despite all evidence to the contrary, Jesus *does* hold all authority and power in his hands. He is YHWH incarnate on earth, and his death *is* in accordance with the divine purposes. God has vindicated the crucified Jesus by raising him from the dead. Christians may be reassured that their sufferings too are within the purposes of a gracious Father and under his control. And the Father will vindicate us too by giving us the new life of the resurrection.

So the New Testament is partly written in order to reassure those early Christians – and us too – that our faith holds water. Even when we are in a tiny minority as Christians, with the masses of our people against us, we can believe in Jesus with total confidence. Even when the media and the world of education firmly oppose Jesus and sneer at our faith, the New Testament stands like an unshakeable bulwark against all assaults. Our faith in Jesus has firm foundations. What a comfort for struggling little churches in modern Europe and for Christians in situations of fierce persecution in Muslim countries, China or other anti-Christian societies. The Christians may feel themselves an insignificant minority with few powerful, wealthy or top-educated adherents, but Jesus is the Messiah and Saviour he claimed to be. He can be trusted.

As we read the New Testament we must never forget that it is written with this aim to encourage Christians who are under siege. Christology has this purpose; it is not just written in order to develop a true theology for the ivory tower. It is a relevant message for new Christians living within a hostile non-Christian society.

Universality

Jesus came to save not only his own Jewish people, but also the Gentiles of all nations. In our generation this statement seems so obvious, for the Christian Church has for centuries consisted largely of Gentiles. To suggest that the Christian faith might only be for Jews would be ridiculous. But the early Church faced an enormous battle on this point.

In Old Testament times, right up to the time of Jesus, God the Creator, the God of Israel, restricted his covenant exclusively to Jews. Gentiles had to become proselytes or God-fearers if they wanted to worship him. As proselytes they had to be circumcised, submit to the Jewish law and thus become members of the people of Israel. While God's kingdom stretched beyond the confines of the Jewish people, membership of the people of Israel was an essential condition for the worship of God. The New Testament Church faced the danger that it too might become just a messianic sect of Judaism. Such ethnic particularism would of course seriously hinder its spread among the Gentiles. As the apostle to the Gentiles, Paul was naturally particularly concerned to prove that outreach to the Gentiles was in accordance with God's purposes. And as the companion of Paul in some of his missionary journeying, Luke too gives considerable priority to this matter. But the theme of the universality of the gospel runs right through the New Testament.

We may notice that the heated New Testament question is whether it is right to evangelise Gentiles and allow them to remain entirely Gentile as Christians. Today the boot has slipped on to the wrong foot. Some more pluralistic Christians are denying the validity of evangelisation among Jewish people, declaring that Jesus is only for Gentiles! The early Christians would have found that extremely strange.

As the history of the early Church unfolded in the second half of the first century, large numbers of Gentiles flooded into the Christian Church. Inevitably Christians were forced to ask themselves serious questions. Had Jesus foreseen this influx of Gentiles? Was it in accordance with the teaching and practice of

Jesus that Gentiles should be evangelised and accepted into the Church? If Gentiles were to be received into the Church, could they remain thoroughly Gentile or must they submit to the Jewish law and be circumcised? If Gentiles were accepted into the Church alongside Jewish believers, how should they inter-relate? Should the Jewish Christians compromise their adherence to the Law or should the Gentiles lose some of their freedom? The New Testament struggles with these issues.

If the early Church had become just a messianic sect of Judaism and remained ethnically narrow, the Christian Church today would never have become the great international body it is.

Because of the context of the first-century religious situation, the New Testament strongly emphasises the universality of the ministry of Jesus and of the Church. The gospel is not only for Jews, but also for Samaritans and Gentiles of all nations. Gentile commentators and preachers have generally underplayed the essential central place given to this universality in the New Testament. As a result, a blinkered ethno-centric faith has plagued the Church, and international mission has not been at the very heart of the life of the Church. It is my prayer that this little book may play a small part in rectifying the situation and giving its readers a truer understanding of Scripture.

1

Matthew and mission: encouraging a minority Church

In the Introduction we have observed that the New Testament Church was a tiny minority in the midst of an unbelieving community. The odds seemed to be stacked against those early Christians.

Matthew wrote his Gospel not only in order to recount an accurate history of the life, relationships and teaching of Jesus, but also specifically to strengthen the faith of the believing community to whom he was writing. And it would seem that he already had his eyes projected forwards to the wider Christian Church which would evolve in the coming years. It is in this context and for this reason that he seeks to demonstrate the validity of Jesus' ministry and to develop the theme of who Jesus really is.

We have noted too that the New Testament Church faced the unexpected situation where the great majority of the people of Israel rejected Jesus as Messiah, while multitudes of Gentiles pressed into the Church with a vital faith and hope in Jesus.

Matthew was writing for Jewish Christians primarily, but nevertheless had to face with them the questions which arose for the Church because of this influx of Gentiles. He particularly emphasises that Jesus himself had prepared the way for the coming of Gentiles into the kingdom of God. Jesus would not have been taken by surprise because of the growing number coming into his Church. As followers of Jesus, therefore, those first disciples of Jesus could accept the new situation with equanimity and welcome their Gentile sisters and brothers as equal members of the body of Christ.

As we look at the topic of 'Matthew and mission', we shall take these two topics in turn and trust the Holy Spirit to increase our understanding of Matthew's Gospel and thus of the word of God for his people even today.

To strengthen disciples' faith

In Britain today people often say, 'I wish I had a faith like yours. It must be a real help in life to have a faith.' But the New Testament is not at all interested in 'faith' or 'a faith' of such an unspecific nature. The heart of true faith lies in a definite relationship with Jesus the Messiah and Saviour. True faith depends on a right understanding of who Jesus really is and what he does. The early Christians, of course, could not possibly doubt the fact of Jesus' existence, but under the pressures of life in an anti-Christian society they needed reassurance of the truth of Jesus as the fulfilment of Old Testament prophecy. While we may not necessarily agree with his undue dependence on sociological analysis or with all the reasons he gives for his assertion, Philip Esler is surely right to point out in his *Community and Gospel in Luke – Acts* (CUP, 1987) that 'The members of his community . . . needed strong assurance that their decision to convert and to adopt a different life-style had been the correct one.' Matthew's community of believers too needed confirmation of Jesus in his multi-faceted roles and titles. So Matthew was not concerned merely to develop an ivory-tower Christology so that the Church might stick firm to a sound theology. He was writing particularly for the sake of his fellow-Christians that his description of Jesus might undergird their faith and keep them strong in their Christian commitment.

The genealogy

With tremendous boldness Matthew starts by declaring that this is 'the book of the genesis of Jesus Christ' (1:1, my literal translation). In this way he refers not only to Genesis 1:1 but also to Genesis 2:4 and 5:1. As the creation account gave the commencement of the development of the world and the outset of human history, so the coming of Jesus Christ saw the beginning of a new era for humanity and the world. The coming of Jesus Christ into this world was not just the story of another human being's birth, but it was a crucial event which changed the whole course of the world. The new creation had burst on to the stage of history.

It is fitting, therefore, that history is divided according to whether it is before or after Christ, BC or AD. Having relatively recently celebrated the turn of the new millennium, we have been reminded that Jesus Christ is the crucial turning point of all history. The secular world may try to avoid what is for them an uncomfortable assertion, but the reality of this fact stares us in the face. The early Christians will also have been reassured by this great truth that Jesus' incarnation is the vital event of history which ushers in a new era. In Jesus there is a new creation, not just for individual believers but indeed for all humanity and for all creation.

Matthew 1:1 gives three further titles to Jesus. He is the Messiah/Christ, the son of David and the son of Abraham. These are repeated at the end of the genealogy in 1:17, but with the further addition of the deportation to Babylon, for the coming of Jesus brings not only salvation but also judgment. Through their rejection of Jesus Israel faced renewed national disaster, a fact which Matthew's readers will have appreciated only too well if indeed this Gospel was written after the Roman sack of Jerusalem, with the destruction of the temple. The message of salvation can only be truly appreciated when it is also contrasted with the fearful nature of God's judgment. Light shows up in its splendour in contrast to darkness. Thus Luther saw the left and right hands of God working together in grace and judgment, the natural work of God ('*opus proprium*') and his unnatural working ('*opus alienum*'). The positive and the negative must be held together in the Christian message.

It was of primary importance for Matthew's readers to be reassured that Jesus was indeed the Messiah/Christ. The Jewish people had been waiting expectantly for their Messiah for century after century. Then in more recent times a variety of false messiahs had appeared briefly on the scene, leading their followers into bitter disillusionment. Already in the first century after Jesus' death, Bar Kochba declared himself to be the Messiah and even received the support of the great Rabbi Akiba. Had it not been for the sure evidence of Jesus' resurrection his disciples could have easily felt that the ignominiously crucified Jesus was perhaps just another false Messiah. So Matthew starts his Gospel with the assertion that Jesus is indeed the Christ. Still today Jewish Christians commonly call him 'Jesus the Messiah', but Matthew leaves out the definite article. Was it that the messiah-ship of Jesus was so assumed that the title 'Christ' had become just a part of Jesus' name? Or was it a Gentile influence which did not appreciate the significance of the title 'Messiah'? In any case, Matthew is presenting his readers with the assurance that Jesus is the long-awaited Messiah. New churches and those in situations of fierce opposition have always throughout history needed such reassurance.

The genealogy introduces Matthew's frequently repeated emphasis on Jesus as the son of David. Just a few verses later the angel repeats this messianic title (1:20). As son of David, Jesus is not only qualified to be the Messiah, but he is also shown to be the king of the kingdom of God. He thus claims for himself all the royal prerogatives of the king of kings. It is through relationship with the king that people may now enter and belong to the kingdom. All the characteristics of the kingdom come under the divine rule of the king – righteousness, justice, peace and joy. The messianic kingdom was also expected to be universal in its scope, including Gentiles of all nations as well as the Jewish people.

For Matthew's Jewish readers it was vitally important that the Messiah was also a direct descendant of 'our father Abraham'. For Jews the figure of Abraham stands supreme as the progenitor of our people. The fact that Jesus is a true son of Abraham gives him acceptable credibility. National identity is still of enormous significance, not only for Jews but for all peoples. As Jesus identifies so clearly with his own Jewish people, so he also gives a model for the whole development of the Christian Church. As far as possible, ambassadors of Christ need to strive to walk in his footsteps of identification, showing that the faith of Jesus is not some foreign exotic but belongs to the very soil of the people.

The climax of the genealogy comes in the shape of a threefold repetition of the number fourteen. This has given rise to various reactions among those who insist on a literalist interpretation of the Bible. Some have sought to justify the historical accuracy of the fourteen generations. Other critics have found proof in it that the Bible is historically inaccurate and untrue. So, for example, my daughter came back from school one day deeply distressed. Her Religious Education teacher had taught the class that the Bible could not be trusted and was not God's word because Matthew 1:17 was patently untrue. At that young age my daughter had no answer to such teaching. I pointed out to her that Jews use numbers not only mathematically but also sometimes with symbolic significance. Matthew was not intending to say that there were exactly fourteen generations between each stage of history. And his original readers would not have understood his words that way.

In Hebrew each letter of the alphabet is given a numerical significance. And the letters forming the name 'David' add up to fourteen. Matthew's threefold usage of the number fourteen therefore highlights that Jesus is the great son of David, the davidic Messiah, the king of kings.

And fourteen is twice seven, which is the number of completion and perfection. Jesus is doubly seven/perfect and indeed three times doubly perfect! Matthew is not only saying that Jesus is the davidic king, but also that he is gloriously and superbly perfect – 3 x 2 x 7.

So Matthew encourages the early Christians to whom he is writing that their faith is not misplaced. Jesus is all that he is cracked up to be – and more!

Saviour

Having repeated the important fact that Jesus' birth is the work of the Holy Spirit (1:18, 20) and therefore not a merely human occurrence, Matthew goes on to stress the name 'Jesus' (1:21, 25). In Hebrew it is the same as 'Joshua' and so may imply that Jesus has come to bring his people into the promised land. They may encounter fierce enemies and endure tremendous battles, but as their leader, Jesus will lead them into all the promises of God.

The name 'Jesus' literally means 'Saviour' and 1:21 develops this thought. While it is true that Jesus saves from sickness and death, from natural disasters and attacks from enemies, the foundational work of salvation refers to the essential reality that Jesus saves from sin. All other outworkings of Jesus' power to save flow out from his deliverance from sin.

In emphasising the word 'he', 1:21 underlines the fact that it is Jesus who saves from sin. Matthew's readers cannot escape the implication that Jesus is the one and only Saviour from sin. In this way the exclusive claims of Jesus counteract any pluralistic philosophy in which all religions have equal validity. An intolerant rejection of all belief in absolute truth (however much it may come in the name of tolerance) becomes unacceptable to the Christian believer in Jesus as the one true Saviour. Christians today struggle to express their faith acceptably in the midst of a society which is supremely tolerant of tolerance, but fearfully intolerant of anything which appears intolerant. But throughout all ages Christians have gloried in the sure knowledge that Jesus is indeed the unique Saviour.

In the Old Testament and in Jewish thought, the word 'people' commonly relates to Israel as the people of God. Matthew's Jewish readers would normally have expected Jesus as Messiah to save 'God's people Israel' from their sins. But now, with the coming of Jesus the Messiah, it is relationship with him which determines our spiritual state. It is *Jesus'* people who enjoy the forgiveness of their sins. Relationship with God as his people is now based on committed faith in Jesus. It is of course open to people of all backgrounds to follow Jesus as Lord and Saviour. Jesus will save 'his people' and they are no longer just the Jewish people of Israel, but may also include people of all ethnic backgrounds. In 26:28 too, forgiveness of sins through the sacrificial death of Jesus is not just for Israel, but for 'many' – a word which has a wider inter-ethnic connotation. As we shall see in more detail below, this very Jewish Gospel has the wider international mission of Jesus very much in its sights.

Immanuel

As I have elaborated more fully in *Matthew and Mission – the Gospel through Jewish Eyes* (Paternoster, 2001), the use of the title 'Immanuel' in Isaiah and Matthew is remarkable. Knowing that the more intimate covenant name for God in the Old Testament is YHWH, we might have expected Jesus to be called 'ImmanuYHWH'/YHWH with us. When we look at John's Gospel it will become evident that Jesus is indeed YHWH/I AM with us. But Matthew quotes Isaiah in showing Jesus to be 'El' with us. And seeing the context of Jesus heralding in the new creation (1:1), we might also have expected him to be 'Immanu-Eloah' or 'Immanu-Elohim', with the early Genesis names for the creator God.

Amazingly and significantly, however, Jesus is also incarnate as 'El' with us. This should immediately face us with the question of who 'El' is. Many of the early Middle Eastern peoples called their high creator deity 'El'. 'El' was introduced into the Old Testament by Melchizedek and thereafter was considered the equivalent of the Hebrew 'Eloah/Elohim'. Presumably the understanding of the character, relationships and working of 'El' needed to be adapted from its pagan background to fit the definite biblical revelation. As English-speaking Christians we shall understand this situation well, for the pre-Christian pagan tribes of Britain called their high creator deity 'God'. When the first Christians came to Britain, they took over this name and adapted the previously pagan tribal understanding of 'God' to fit the biblical revelation in Christ.

The use of 'El' has important missiological significance. It gives a biblical undergirding to the practice of taking over the high creator deities of other religions and then adapting the understanding of their nature to fit the character of the biblical Elohim/YHWH who is revealed to us in Jesus Christ. It will be right therefore to say that Jesus is 'Allah with us' despite the background of wrong Muslim understanding of the nature of Allah. And in today's mission situation in Britain it will still be right to call the creator 'God' despite the gravely inadequate and false views of God prevalent in our wider society.

We need at this stage to note, however, that in both the Old and New Testaments no compromise was permitted with the shrine idol deities like the Baalim or the personalised Greek and Roman gods. Likewise in early Britain, 'God' was brought over into the Christian faith, but Wodun, Thor and the other idol gods were forbidden and their shrines utterly destroyed. In many non-Christian contexts today Christian mission will have to stand against the pluralistic tolerance current in the western world. No compromise with the worship of idols and shrine deities can be allowed among people who call themselves Christian. God himself repudiates all such pagan religion.

The kingdom

It is my privilege to speak at many Christian conferences. Frequently the people there go away with a renewed sense of the glory of the Lord and feel spiritually refreshed. Sometimes I feel it right to warn them that a spiritual 'high' can easily be followed by the trough of failure or demonic opposition.

So it was with Jesus at the outset of his ministry. He must have been excited at his baptism, with the Spirit of God descending on him like a dove and the heavenly voice affirming 'this is my beloved Son, with whom I am well pleased' (3:17, RSV). But this led straight into the wilderness experience of forty days fasting and satanic temptation. Matthew links the baptism with the temptation by repeating 'the Spirit' (3:16; 4:1) and 'the Son' (3:17; 4:3; 4:6). So the commencement of Jesus' ministry starts with God's clear word of call and favour as well as Satan's determined opposition. As Christians follow Jesus in Christian mission we may expect something of the same.

When the period of temptation came to its end and Jesus heard of John's arrest (4:12), he withdrew to Galilee. With its considerable Gentile population Galilee was more friendly than the vehemently hostile Judea where both John the Baptist and Jesus himself would be killed. In the next chapter we shall develop further the theme that it was 'Galilee of the Gentiles' where Jesus first preached the kingdom.

The suffering of John leads to Jesus' declaration: 'Repent, for the kingdom of heaven is at hand' (4:17, RSV). In Jewish thought as reflected also in the New Testament, the suffering of God's people is the unavoidable prelude to the coming of God's kingdom. Without preceding suffering there can be no kingdom. Death precedes life, the resurrection can only come after the cross. In Christian mission this principle needs to be remembered. Christian workers who want the kingdom of God to come and who pray 'thy kingdom come' must be prepared for suffering as the precondition.

In our contemporary Christian teaching the kingdom is often

associated either with the demand for social justice or with the practice of miraculous signs and wonders with the defeat of demonic powers. While both these emphases contain considerable truth, both seem to neglect the call to suffering as the means towards the coming of the kingdom. In fact, many younger Christians can stumble in their faith when suffering afflicts them.

In Jewish and biblical thought the kingdom of God is also inseparably associated with righteousness. In the teaching of the rabbis it is assumed that righteousness is the precondition for the coming of the kingdom. When Israel fulfils all the commandments, they say, then the kingdom will come. Jesus reverses the order. Because the kingdom is here, he exhorts his followers therefore to repent and turn to righteousness. So the coming of the kingdom ushers in a new growth in righteousness and holiness. The sign of genuine kingdom life is repentance which leads to holiness of life.

As Jesus set out on his mission his first act was to call the first four of his future band of twelve disciples. They were to become the leaders among his disciples, with a particularly close relationship with him (cf. M. Goldsmith, *Jesus and His Relationships*, Paternoster, 2000). There is a direct line of continuity from the Old Testament to its climax in the person of John the Baptist. Jesus picks up John's message of repentance and the kingdom (3:2; 4:17). Both will also suffer death at the hands of the authorities. Then the line of continuity continues from Jesus to his followers and thus on through the early Church to Christians throughout the ages.

The call of the disciples is first to 'follow' Jesus and then also to be 'fishers' (4:19). When we first went to Indonesia we were surprised to find that the word 'follow' was constantly used by the churches with and under which we worked. They did not commonly talk about being converted or born again, but emphasised following Jesus. By this was meant that people should base their lives on Jesus as their model. Then too they should be obedient to him as Lord of their lives. And finally, 'follow' implied an intimate relationship of trust, as between a shepherd and his sheep. Mission from the first century until today always has this aim, that people should come to Jesus and follow him.

Everyone who follows Jesus is also called to become 'fishers'. By various means we aim to bring people into faith in Jesus and thus incorporate them into his Church. Sadly the Church is often so involved in keeping the aquarium of its own congregation that it has little active involvement in fishing out in the oceans. Of course, it is of vital importance that the teaching and pastoral ministry among the faithful should not be neglected. But the goal of evangelistic mission must remain in the forefront of our church life. Congregations need to rethink and restructure in order to become effective missionary congregations. Life in God's kingdom and discipleship of Jesus must involve a heartfelt concern for witness and outreach in the world.

Jesus has authority

As Jesus set out on his ministry he began to preach that the kingdom of heaven was now near (4:17). But the early disciples must have wondered. Was he really the heavenly king, the davidic Messiah? As the king, did he demonstrate appropriate kingly and messianic authority?

Immediately Jesus began his preaching of the kingdom he called the first four of his twelve disciples to follow him and become 'fishers of men and women' (4:19). Did Jesus really have the right to call people to follow him in self-sacrificing discipleship? What right did he have to send his followers out in costly witness and mission?

These questions must also have pressed in upon those first disciples in the early Christian Church for which Matthew was writing. So Matthew develops the theme of Jesus' evident authority in word, in deed and in the call to mission.

In word (chapters 5 to 7)
Some commentators have noted how Matthew's Gospel contains five blocks of teaching material, paralleling the five books of

Moses. In this way it seems that Matthew was demonstrating that Jesus came as the second Moses with all his teaching authority. Just as Moses gave the people of Israel God's word concerning the patterns of life which are pleasing to the holy God, so also Jesus gives principles for life in God's kingdom.

He starts by teaching his disciples the way of blessing/ happiness in the kingdom. The normal patterns of human society are reversed in the kingdom. Happiness and blessing do not come through prosperity and success, but rather to the poor in spirit, those who mourn, the meek and those who hunger and thirst in their desire for righteousness. Indeed, the climax of the Beatitudes asserts that the kingdom belongs to those who are persecuted because of righteousness and those who suffer insults and slander for Jesus' sake. A great reward in heaven awaits those who suffer persecution because of their witness to Jesus – what a comfort that must have been to the persecuted Christians of the early centuries of church history! And indeed it remains a word of strong encouragement to persecuted Christians in many parts of the world today. Matthew's threefold repetition of the word 'persecute' (5:10–12) stresses the fact that it is in situations of such suffering that followers of Jesus can rejoice and be glad as they experience the true blessing of life in God's kingdom.

Having emphasised the poverty and humble meekness of Christian discipleship, Matthew proceeds to underline the word 'you' (5:13, 14) in his affirmation that Jesus' followers are the salt of the earth and the light of the world. In his grace God uses even inadequate people like those first disciples to bring glory to our heavenly Father. Through their 'good deeds' light will come to 'the world'. Matthew's use of the words 'the world' and 'everyone' implies that God's glory will spread beyond the confines of Israel to the whole world.

Jesus goes on to teach that he has come to bring the Law and the Prophets to their fulfilment. He has not come to repeal or abolish the word of God through Moses, but rather to bring it to its climactic fulfilment. In saying this, Jesus claims authority to bring to the world the fulness of God's Law. So he says again and again, 'you have heard that it was said . . .' and then with divine authority he adds, 'but I tell you . . .' As the new Moses, Jesus has the authority to bring the final Law of God.

The repeated words 'I tell you . . .' reveal that Jesus has the right to bring the final word of authority. He is not just, like Moses, a messenger to bring the word of the Lord. The Law-giving authority of God himself resides in Jesus. So he is not only the second Moses, but also the very incarnation of YHWH himself.

The climax of the Sermon on the Mount is the call to 'hear these words of mine and put them into practice' (7:24) and thus to 'do the will of my Father who is in heaven' (7:21). Jesus' words carry such authority that life in the kingdom of God is characterised by hearing his teaching and acting accordingly. Relationship to the creator God of Israel is now dependent on our attitude to Jesus, his teaching and therefore our obedience to him.

We may note that faith in Jesus is not just an emotional relationship of love, but specifically means such attention to Jesus' preaching and teaching that we live in accordance with his word. So Jesus declares that merely worshipping him and calling him 'Lord, Lord' is not adequate for entry into the kingdom of heaven. Likewise even the exercise of a prophetic gift in his name or performing miracles and driving out demons may still elicit the Lord's grave words: 'I never knew you. Away from me, you evildoers' (7:21–3). Christians' words must be matched by their deeds of holiness in obedience to Jesus.

It may be unfashionable in the modern age to underline the vital importance of words, but God reveals himself through his word and Jesus judges our discipleship according to whether we hear and obey his word. Thus faith is also inseparably linked to good works in accordance with Jesus' teaching. Both Paul and James in their letters would also stress this combination of faith and works. A faith which does not lead to holy righteousness is indeed dead.

So Jesus brings this block of teaching to an end with the story of the wise man who built his house on the rock, while the foolish man built his on the sand. With this story Jesus reveals that the solid and true foundation for life in his kingdom is 'hearing these words of mine and doing them' (7:24). So hearing and doing go hand in hand. Everyone needs an underlying philosophy or ideology which will act as their foundation for life and determine their beliefs, thoughts and practices. In the heyday of Communism, atheistic Marxism underlay every aspect of life in those countries, but with the demise of Communism people lack a foundational ideology and purpose. The western world also swims aimlessly without the strong anchor of a faith which governs everything from politics to art, from education to economics. Jesus confidently declares that the one true foundation for building our lives is in hearing *his* words and doing them.

Jesus' bold confidence is claiming absolute authority. It is *his* words which form the foundation for life. It is obedience to *him* that determines whether we are doing the will of his Father in heaven and so have entered his kingdom. No wonder that Chapter 7 concludes with the statement that the crowds 'were amazed at his teaching, because he taught as one who had authority' (7:28, 29).

So the early Christians for whom Matthew was writing will have been encouraged. Even if the rabbis and other leaders of Israel contradicted and attacked the Christian faith, it remained true that Jesus' teaching was the fulfilment of everything in the Old Testament, and its truth was the reliable foundation for life in God's kingdom. Jesus' words did indeed carry authority whatever other people might say. Christians can go out in mission with this confidence.

In deed (chapters 8 and 9)

Having shown Jesus' authority in word, Matthew proceeds to demonstrate his authority in deed. Jesus heals a man with leprosy (8:1–4), the servant of a Gentile Roman centurion (8:5–13) and then Peter's mother-in-law (8:14–17). Thus Jesus shows his loving concern for the despised of society – a leper, a Gentile and a woman (even a mother-in-law!). In this way he gives renewed value to those who were considered beyond the pale of respectable religious life. Jesus has the authority, as well as the love, to do this. As the prophet Isaiah said, 'He took up our infirmities and carried our diseases' (8:17; Isa. 53:4). As a despised minority the early Christians will have been touched by the assurance of Jesus' power and by his active concern for the 'little people'.

But they may have been surprised at the way Jesus appeared to court antagonism from the Jewish leaders. He touched the man with leprosy and Peter's mother-in-law. In those days it was not acceptable for a man actually to touch a woman or a person with leprosy, but Jesus reaches out beyond the confines of such rules in order to show his love as he works the miracle of healing. He will have provoked even worse hatred among the Jewish authorities by his astonished comments on observing the re-markable faith of the Gentile centurion. He declared that at the messianic feast of Abraham 'many will come from the east and the west' while 'the subjects of the kingdom will be thrown outside, into the darkness' (8:11–12). The kingdom will no longer be just for Israel and those Gentile proselytes who join themselves to the people of God, but multitudes of Gentiles will sit at Abraham's table.

Before proceeding to tell of further miracles which demon-strated the power and authority of Jesus, Matthew interposes some verses (8:18–22) which show the cost of wholehearted discipleship. Following Jesus involves incurring the fierce opposi-tion of non-believers, so Jesus warns his disciples that they too must be willing to suffer loss of comfort and home. Our love for Jesus must be greater even than the supreme family responsibility of burying a parent. With Jesus there can be no half-hearted discipleship.

Having shown his power over nature by stilling the storm (8:23–7), Jesus crossed over into Gentile territory and delivered two men from demonic powers (8:28–34), thus showing that the kingdom of God had now irrupted into the world. It was commonly accepted that with the coming of the kingdom Satan would be defeated and his power broken by the Spirit of God. Knowing that the defeat of demonic powers was a sign of the end time, the demon-possessed men call out to Jesus, 'Have you come here to torture us *before the appointed time?*' But they were to learn that with the coming of Jesus the end time has arrived, and so he casts out the demons.

Jesus also claims the right to forgive sins and heals the paralytic to prove it (9:1–8). It is in this context of the demonstration of Jesus' authority in every area of life that Jesus called Matthew to follow him. As the call of the first four disciples was linked to their commission to be 'fishers of men', so now Matthew's call is in the context of Jesus eating with sinners. Jesus' ministry was to bring mercy not to the righteous but to sinners. And as Jesus' follower this calling extended also to Matthew, and on to the Church throughout history.

What a Saviour who brings God's mercy in the forgiveness of our sin! No wonder mourning and fasting give way to rejoicing! The kingdom of God has come, the new creation has burst on to the scene of history. Those who 'kneel before him' and have faith in him will find healing and life from the dead (9:18–26). The blind will see, the deaf will speak and the demon-possessed will be delivered (9:27–34). Followers of Jesus who have experienced their eyes and mouths being opened cannot but go out and 'spread the news about him all over the region' (9:31). However much the leaders of society may falsely accuse and criticise him, common people will declare with amazement that the power, authority and merciful love of Jesus are unique (9:33).

Christians are not only called to stand still in wondering amazement at the supreme splendour of Jesus. Awe-filled worship must lead on to mission. Just as Jesus himself went around teaching, preaching the good news and healing people with deep compassion for the crowds, so too his followers are to pray that the Lord will send out workers into his harvest. And we dare not pray in such a way without being ourselves obedient to his call to witness and mission.

In sending into mission (chapter 10)

At the outset of his sending the twelve out in mission, Jesus passes on to them his authority. This includes the ministry of casting out evil spirits and healing the sick. The heart of their witness is in preaching the kingdom, restricting their ministry at this stage to Israel rather than going to the Samaritans or the Gentiles. But actually their testimony will also reach the Gentiles as well as the Jewish authorities (10:18).

God's mission starts with his people in the Old Testament and climaxes in the ministry of Jesus himself. Jesus then passes on his calling to his disciples and thus on to his people throughout history.

So Jesus has no hesitation in calling his disciples to witness for him in mission despite the inevitable persecution and opposition this will arouse. He has the authority to expect his followers to commit themselves without reservation to his service, whatever that may cost. Nervous Christians in European countries today may need to be encouraged to submit to Jesus' authority in calling his followers to active outgoing evangelistic mission.

'Who do you say I am?' (16:15)

In Matthew 15 Jesus responds to the great faith of the Gentile Canaanite woman (21–8) and feeds a Gentile crowd (32–8), thus provoking questioning opposition among the Jewish leaders (16:1–12). This situation brings to the forefront the vital question of the disciples' attitude to Jesus. Have they grasped the reality of who Jesus actually is? Can Jesus therefore now move on towards his death in the confidence that his disciples are ready to continue his mission of bringing salvation to all nations everywhere? Or would the disciples be influenced by the unbelief and false teaching of the Pharisees and Sadducees?

Caesarea Philippi is a turning point in the narrative of Jesus' life. He starts by asking his disciples, 'Who do people say the Son of Man is?' He then quickly proceeds to the key question, 'Who do *you* say I am?' By inspiration of the Father in heaven Peter leads the other disciples in the confession, 'You are the Christ/ Messiah, the Son of the living God.' It is difficult to know exactly what Peter understood at that early stage by the title 'Son of God'. In the Old Testament the people of Israel were called the 'children of God' and in Ezekiel the title 'son of God' is just a way of saying 'a person'. So it had no background meaning of deity. But by the time Matthew was writing, this title had come to carry new significance. It now pointed to the deity of Jesus as God incarnate. It is quite possible, therefore, that Peter did not understand the vital significance of his own declaration that Jesus was the Son of God. But Matthew and his readers will have nodded their heads in agreement that Jesus is God incarnate. And Peter will certainly have known the importance of his confession that Jesus was the Christ/Messiah, the long-awaited Saviour for his people.

Immediately following this interaction with Peter, Jesus begins to reveal to his disciples the fact that he will go to Jerusalem, suffer death there and then be raised again to life. By the use of the word 'must' (16:21) Jesus demonstrates that his impending death and resurrection are not historical accidents, but are the necessary fulfilment of Old Testament prophecy and of the purposes of God for the salvation of the world. Peter showed his unspiritually natural desire for comfort, success and well-being by resisting Jesus' warnings concerning the necessity of the cross. Suffering does not come easily to any of us, but taking up the cross and following Jesus is an essential ingredient of Christian discipleship (16:24). And true Christian mission will always involve suffering. In suffering, Christians walk in the footsteps of Jesus and find the solace of fellowship with him.

Matthew continues the story with his account of the Trans-figuration (17:1–11), when the disciples saw with their own eyes the glory of Jesus. They not only saw his face shining like the sun and his clothes gleaming white like dazzling light, but also heard the heavenly voice echoing the words at his baptism. God himself testified that Jesus is his beloved Son, with whom he is well pleased. And the appearance of Jesus together with Moses and Elijah underlines the fact that Jesus stands in the direct line of the Law and the Prophets in continuity with the purposes of God in the history of Israel. For Jewish believers this was and is vitally important.

So Matthew's Gospel bolsters the faith of disciples of Jesus surrounded by a hostile sea of unbelief. They can be reassured in their call to witness, for Jesus is indeed the true son of Abraham, of Moses and of King David. He is YHWH and Immanuel present among us. Jesus' followers may waver in their faith, feeling that they are the only soldiers in step. But they can be reassured that Jesus really is the God-sent Messiah and glorious Son of God who fulfils all the Old Testament's prophetic expectations of the one who was to come. Jesus is the 3 x 2 x 7 son of David and Messiah, the all-glorious king of God's kingdom. He has authority of word and deed, calling his followers to be 'fishers of men' and to go out in mission with his own delegated authority, not only to preach the kingdom but also to cast out demons, to raise the dead and to heal. In committing themselves to him his followers become 'his people' and can have confidence that he 'saves his people from their sins'.

The ensuing chapters in Matthew's Gospel will highlight the growing opposition and foreshadow the fierce persecution which Jesus' followers will suffer in their witness for him. Although this antagonism will culminate for Jesus in death on the cross, that is not the end of the story. God will raise Jesus from the dead and the risen Christ will accompany his people as they accept his authority and obey his commission to 'go and make disciples of all nations' (28:19).

2

Matthew and mission: universality

Right at the outset of Matthew's Gospel the genealogy of Jesus already foreshadows the wide ministry of Jesus to those who were usually considered to be beyond the pale. Unlike the normal genealogies of that period of history, Matthew notes that through his family background Jesus identifies not just with the righteous of Israel, but particularly with the socially excluded of all nations and backgrounds. Thus the genealogy includes people with sinful connections (e.g. Tamar, Rahab, King David through his murder and adultery, as well as evil kings like Manasseh). It also specifically lists women – Tamar, Rahab, Ruth, Bathsheba and finally Mary herself. And the very Jewish Gospel of Matthew further notes that Jesus in his genealogy has Gentile connections – Tamar, Ruth and probably Bathsheba, the wife of Uriah the Hittite.

When Matthew proceeds to demonstrate Jesus' authority in deed (chapters 8 and 9), he again points out how Jesus showed his loving acceptance of the socially excluded. The first three miracles of healing were for a leprosy sufferer, the servant of a Gentile centurion and Peter's mother-in-law, a woman. In 8:28–

9:8 Jesus proceeds to bring healing salvation to two demon-possessed men and to a paralytic, to whom he declares, 'Your sins are forgiven.' Salvation is the principal purpose of Jesus' ministry to the outcast. So in the final events of the cross and resurrection Matthew repeatedly uses the word 'save' (e.g. Matt. 27:40–3). Again, in a very sexist society he emphasises that it was women who 'were there' with and for Jesus in his ultimate need on the cross (27:55, 56) and in Matthew's Gospel the two Marys were the only witnesses of the resurrection. While the angel instructs them to 'tell' the other disciples about the resurrection, the risen Jesus changes the word and instructs them to 'announce' the resurrection (28:10, my literal translation). The word 'announce' (*apaggeilate*) has the sense of verbal proclamation. It is significant, therefore, that two women were the first preachers of the good news of Jesus' resurrection. Unbiased translations ought to make this change clear, whatever their views on women's ministry. In passing it should be noted too that the New Testament does not distinguish between pulpit preaching and the everyday proclamation of the gospel across the garden fence.

The crucifixion also sees a Gentile Roman centurion confessing that Jesus is the Son of God (27:54). So Matthew underlines the wide ministry of Jesus to sinners and the socially excluded, to women and to Gentiles. This demonstrates the wide scope of 'his people' (1:21) to whom Jesus brings forgiveness of sins.

But Jesus' loving concern particularly reaches out to the 'little ones', a description which refers to those who follow Jesus. His disciples are also described as *oligopistoi*, or 'little-faith-people'. Just as Israel was called to be God's chosen people because it was the least among the nations, so also Jesus delights to call to himself the insignificant and the outcast. In particular, Matthew stresses that the kingdom and Jesus himself may be rejected by the leaders of Israel, but he still calls Jewish 'little ones' and Gentiles to be his followers.

The vineyard (21:28–46) and the marriage feast (22:1–14)

In these two parables the vineyard is removed from the hands of the former tenants and given to 'other tenants'. Likewise at the wedding banquet the rightfully invited guests are destroyed and 'did not deserve to come', so the wedding hall was filled with all sorts of other people. Jesus makes the meaning very clear. In 22:7 he pointedly refers to the anger of the king, who therefore sends his army to destroy 'those murderers' and burn their city. Those who heard Jesus' prophetic words will surely have remembered them very clearly a few years later when the Romans defeated Israel, murdered large multitudes of the people and destroyed the city of Jerusalem with its temple. And Matthew's readers must certainly have applied this verse to those historical events.

The destruction of Israel and the temple is linked in the parables with the in-gathering of a great variety of ordinary people off the street. Not only the 'good' were brought in, but also the 'bad' (22:10). The 'chosen' are clearly distinguished from those who were 'invited' – the final verse of the section and the punch-line of these two parables. Israel and her leaders were invited in to God's covenant and kingdom, but refused to wear the 'wedding clothes' and were therefore thrown out 'into the darkness, where there will be weeping and gnashing of teeth' (22:13). Likewise in the first parable, the original tenants beat, killed and stoned the landowner's servants, finally murdering his son. In consequence the owner of the vineyard will 'bring those wretches to a wretched end' and rent the vineyard to other tenants.

In the Old Testament the vineyard is a picture of Israel, so the meaning is very obvious to the original audience and readers. Israel has consistently rejected and even murdered God's prophets. And now too they will crucify his Son. Therefore 'the kingdom of God will be taken away from you and given to a people who will produce its fruit' (21:43). The use of the word *ethnei*, 'people', has definite Gentile implications.

Do these parables therefore teach a 'replacement theology' in which all Israel is rejected and the kingdom now given to the Gentile Church? While such an understanding of the New Testament is often taught in Gentile Christian churches today, we have to reject it. Matthew always has a threefold division of Israel in his mind. The Pharisees, Sadducees and other leaders of Israel are the 'baddies' who oppose and reject Jesus. With them are also allied the Roman Gentile authorities, and Matthew therefore does not hesitate to use the word 'Gentile' in a pejorative sense sometimes. In clear distinction from this first grouping stand the disciples and other followers of Jesus. They are closely linked to Jesus and he looks to them for the continuation of his ministry of salvation after his death, resurrection and ascension. Between these two groupings are the amorphous 'crowds'/'multitudes' who waver between joining the followers of Jesus and siding with Israel's leaders in rejecting and crucifying him. The two parables of the vineyard and the wedding banquet therefore only teach the rejection of Jesus' enemies in the leadership of Israel plus those crowds which side with them. But in 21:46 Matthew makes a clear distinction between the enemies of Jesus and the crowds who believed him to be a prophet. Israel always has a remnant who remain faithful to God's covenant of righteousness and who follow his Messiah, Jesus. So the new 'people' of God includes the believing remnant of Israel, but now embraces Gentiles also. Jesus' salvation is for Jew and Gentile alike, for every nation and people.

In this message Matthew is closely related to the message of the prophets, particularly Jeremiah. They repeatedly preached a message of judgment on the people of Israel, but also rejoiced in the fact of a faithful remnant who ultimately would find the fullness of life through the climactic unique Remnant, the Servant Messiah himself.

It is noteworthy in these parables that the initiative for choosing his people lies definitely in the hands of God. He it is who gives the kingdom of God to whom he will. He chooses to whom he will now rent his vineyard. Likewise it is the king who sends out his servants to gather in the people from off the streets. He chooses ordinary people to become the elect of God. The new tenants must have wondered why the landowner had particularly chosen them. The new guests at the wedding feast must also have been amazed that the king wanted them at his banquet. This is underlined by Matthew, who places the 'bad' before the 'good' (22:10) – why does the NIV reverse the order?! God himself has the final choice of who will be at the messianic banquet, the table of Abraham. What an amazing reality that God has chosen little people like us! No Christian can ever understand why God should want them, but we can only thank God for his grace.

Grace and election must lead to obedient righteousness in the service of the king. The new tenants will give the landowner 'his share of the crop at harvest time' (21:41). They will be a people who will 'produce the fruit of the kingdom' (21:43). Those who 'did not deserve to come' lost their opportunity to attend the eschatological banquet, but the wedding hall was filled with guests who did wear the wedding clothes which symbolise righteousness.

The chief priests and Pharisees knew that Jesus was talking about them (21:45) and so searched for an opportunity to arrest him. Likewise, after the parable of the wedding banquet the Pharisees planned how they could 'trap him in his words' (22:15). Jesus' teaching provokes fierce opposition and his followers should not fear to follow in his footsteps.

Jesus feeds the Gentiles (15:10–16:4)

Before expounding 15:10–16:4 it is important to see this section in its context. In chapter 14 Jesus hears the heart-rending news of the murder of John the Baptist. In the Gospels, what John preaches Jesus also preaches – 'Repent, for the kingdom of heaven is near.' Likewise what happens to John is a sign of what will befall Jesus. John's murder therefore brings home to Jesus his own impending suffering and death. He felt the urgent need to get alone with his Father as he faced the future. Surely this reminds us as Christians of our need to have time alone with our Father when we face times of difficulty or suffering.

Jesus was too well known to escape the crowds and they followed him on foot around the lake to where he was headed in a boat (14:13). Jesus showed no impatience that his plans of solitude with the Father were frustrated, but showed 'compassion' (cf. 9:36; 18:27) on the crowds. Again, Christians may take Jesus' compassion as a model. When faced with crowds at the supermarket or in the rush hour, it is better to have compassion than to exercise the elbows and the car-horn! And Jesus felt sympathy not only for individuals, but also for the masses of a crowd. He not only felt pity for them as harassed sheep without a shepherd, but he did something for them. He healed their sick.

It seems clear that this was a Jewish crowd and it is noteworthy that the disciples took the initiative in coming to Jesus on their behalf. They feared lest the crowds faint from hunger, and so they requested Jesus to 'send the crowds away' to get some food. When Jesus is faced with a Gentile crowd in the district of Tyre and Sidon (15:21–8) it is he who takes the initiative. He goes to the disciples, saying, 'I have compassion . . . I do not want to send them away hungry' (15:32). With the foreign Gentile crowd the disciples show little concern, replying to Jesus without enthusiasm, 'Where could we get enough bread in this remote place to feed such a crowd?' (15:33). Followers of Jesus are not immune from the temptation to be ethnocentric, with a blinkered vision which is only interested in our own nation and people.

Jesus must have horrified his disciples with his apparently unduly simple response, 'They do not need to go away. You give them something to eat.' My wife and I now have some fellow-feeling for the disciples in their reactions to Jesus' words, for we recently rejoiced in our son's wedding in north-east India. Seven thousand people attended and we observed the massive work involved in cooking the wedding reception meal for such a crowd – 1.8 tons of rice, eight pigs and eight cows were consumed! How pathetic the disciples' words sound! 'We have here only five loaves of bread and two fish' (Matt. 14:17) for the five thousand, and seven loaves and 'a few small fish' (Matt. 15:34) for the four thousand – and it may be assumed the fish were no whales!

But Jesus multiplies the totally inadequate resources of the disciples, so that the crowd eat until they can eat no more. How typical of Jesus! He delights to take our meagre gifts and talents to meet the needs of the crowds. Little people can go into mission with confidence. God will turn our pathetic inadequacy into his means of pouring out his salvation with such lavish generosity that people will overflow with God's superabundant grace.

In 14:19, Matthew uses the words of the institution of the Lord's Supper – Jesus took, gave thanks, broke and gave. And they 'all ate'. In the context of John's death Jesus has his own death in mind. As he feeds the crowds, he is thinking not just of supplying their material needs with bread and fish, but also of supplying their spiritual need for salvation through his atoning death.

The moral is clear. The Christian Church is called to feed the world's crowds with bread and fish, as also with the good news of the forgiveness of sins through Jesus' sacrificial death for us.

In 14:20 the disciples picked up twelve basketfuls of broken pieces. When Jesus has fed the second crowd in the Gentile area they gather seven basketfuls. In Jewish thought, twelve is the number representing the people of Israel, with their twelve tribes. It is significant that Jesus evidently had this usage of numbers in mind also when he chose twelve disciples, showing that his followers stand in direct continuity with the Old Testament people of Israel. On the other hand, seven is the number which represents fullness or completion. It therefore signifies not just Israel but the totality of humanity from all races. Jesus feeds the twelve and the seven, Jews and Gentiles of all peoples.

Later, Jesus asked them how many basketfuls they picked up when he fed the five thousand. They answered, 'Twelve.' And how many basketfuls did they gather when he fed the four thousand? 'Seven,' they replied. And he then said, 'Do you still not understand?' (16:9). It was commonly accepted that in the messianic banquet at the table of Abraham, people from every nation would sit and eat. The feeding of crowds of Jews and of Gentiles was a messianic sign related to the end-time banquet. That is why the Pharisees and Sadducees demand 'a sign from heaven' (16:1) after Jesus has fed the Gentile crowd.

Good news for the Gentiles

The sequence of events is significant after the feeding of the Jewish crowd in 14:13–21. Jesus sets out in a boat to cross the lake en route to the Gentile territory of Gennesaret. It is sometimes pointed out that when Jesus attempts to go into Gentile territory, he often faces demonic opposition. This is particularly true of Mark's account of Jesus' life, but less true of Matthew's Gospel. On this occasion, however, Jesus is attacked by a fierce storm with mountainous waves and violent wind. Matthew knew that in Jewish law a witness is only valid if two witnesses agree together. He therefore often has two parallel stories, and Jesus' miracles relate to two demoniacs, two blind men, etc. In the two stories of Jesus being assailed by a storm on the lake, there is growth in the disciples' faith. In 8:27 the disciples were amazed at his power and asked, 'What kind of man is this?' But in 14:33 they 'worshipped him, saying "truly you are the Son of God" '. Amazement becomes worship and questioning gives way to a confident confession of faith.

Both stories are followed by accounts of Jesus going to Gentile territory and working miracles on behalf of the people. In chapter 8 he casts out demons, in chapter 14 he heals the sick. This emphasis on Jesus' ministry to Gentiles introduces chapter 15.

In 15:10–20 Jesus teaches that uncleanness stems from the heart, from inner motives and desires. It does not come from what goes into the mouth, but what comes out from it. Many

Christians still need to understand this principle, for Pharisaic legalism easily intrudes into the Christian Church. Mission among Gentiles requires the breakdown of externalism in our faith if it is to relate effectively.

This is followed in 15:21–8 by one individual Gentile coming to Jesus. Although the Canaanite woman calls him by the title 'Son of David', he still seems to push her away. He states baldly to her that he is sent only to the lost sheep of Israel. It was, of course, true that until the Old Testament was fulfilled Jesus could not move forward to the wider Gentile ministry which would open up for his followers after his death and resurrection. Yet the Gentile woman is not put off by his rejection of her request. She persists, crying out, 'Lord, help me!' He still refuses to minister on her behalf, replying, 'It is not right to take the children's bread and toss it to their dogs.' By the word 'children' Jesus obviously refers to the children of Israel, whereas 'dogs' was an epithet used sometimes for the Gentiles. But finally her persistent faith in the face of such seemingly steadfast rejection yields fruit. Jesus marvels at her tremendous faith and grants her request. Thus he brings healing to one individual Gentile.

This story of the Canaanite woman leads into the feeding of the Gentile crowd in 15:29–39. When we look at the Acts of the Apostles we shall see a close parallel in the breaking down of externalistic legalism in Peter's vision (Acts 10:9–16), which is followed by the coming to Peter and thus to Jesus of the one individual Gentile, Cornelius. This in turn leads into the wider Gentile mission in the rest of the book of Acts.

The climax to this section in Matthew comes in 16:1–4. By what authority does Jesus feed Jewish and Gentile crowds, thus setting himself up as the Messiah? They demand a sign from heaven, not just an earthly sign like giving food to crowds. Aid agencies can do that without any pretence of being the Messiah – if one ignores the fact that Jesus fed the crowds by a miracle! Jesus, however, refuses to give them any sign except 'the sign of Jonah'. Jesus uses the sign of Jonah more than once. Sometimes it refers to the days and nights in the fish's stomach and thus to his own death and resurrection. But here in Matthew 16 it is in the context of feeding a Gentile crowd. Jonah is the one Old Testament prophet who is sent to preach to Gentiles. Through his preaching the Gentile city of Nineveh repented and was saved. Jesus too, as the Messiah, has come to 'save the Gentiles from their sins' (cf. 1:21).

So the ministry of Jesus relates both to Jews and to Gentiles of all peoples. And it is right in the early Church that the gospel should be preached to Gentiles as well as Jews. Gentiles may indeed be accepted into the Church without becoming prose-lytes and so becoming little Jews. And the Church today is challenged to face its responsibility to follow in Jesus' footsteps, feeding the crowds of Jews and Gentiles of all races with both physical and spiritual food.

The gospel must be preached

Considerable debate has raged around Jesus' extremely negative words concerning Jewish proselytism (23:15). This verse forms part of Jesus' denunciation of the scribes and Pharisees with a list of seven 'Woe to you . . .' The number clearly signifies the terrible fullness of their sin, which even in that generation would experience appalling judgment (23:36). Jesus' final words, how-ever, not only weep over the desolation which is coming upon the holy city of Jerusalem, but also have the mitigating promise that he is coming back. And they will greet him with the words, 'Blessed is he who comes in the name of the Lord'.

Some Christian pastors today use the zealous witness of Jehovah's Witnesses or Muslims as a means of urging their congregations to share their faith more openly and boldly. So one might have expected Jesus to urge his followers to emulate the Pharisees' zeal in spreading the knowledge of God among the Gentile nations. But actually he denounces such active proselytising because it 'shuts the kingdom of heaven in people's faces and does not let them in', thus making people 'twice as much a child of hell as you are' – strong words indeed! The New

Testament stands firmly against its contemporary danger of the Christian Church becoming just a messianic sect of Judaism, in which Gentile converts would have to be circumcised, follow the Jewish law and join themselves to Israel. It therefore avoids all possible association with Jewish proselytism.

But the outgoing preaching of the gospel remains of vital importance in the life of the Church. Jesus sends his disciples out in mission in chapter 10, and when facing the end of his life on earth he underlines it: 'This gospel of the kingdom will be preached in the whole world as a testimony to all nations.' Worldwide evangelism is therefore essential. Only when the gospel has been preached to all nations everywhere will the end come. God's chosen ones will be gathered from all corners of the globe (24:31). In the final judgment 'all the nations will be gathered before him' (25:32). So the prayer 'Thy kingdom come' includes the necessity of international mission outreach.

In the lead-up to the cross a woman anoints Jesus with expensive perfume to show her love for him. In this way she 'prepared him for burial' (26:12). When she was criticised for her apparently wasteful extravagance, Jesus solemnly affirms: 'Wherever this gospel is preached throughout the world, what she has done will also be told.' In passing he thus assumes that the gospel must indeed be preached all over the world. Christian churches easily become narrowly self-centred, navel-gazing and ethnocentric, with little interest in wider mission. We need this reminder.

The climax of the Gospel (28:16–20)

Matthew concludes his Gospel with the bracketing structure of an *inclusio*. As Jesus began his ministry in Galilee of the Gentiles, so now it concludes with Galilee. And as his ministry began with the emphasis of his authority as the law-giving second Moses (chapters 5–7), so at the end he delivers his final command with authority from a mountain. In chapter 1 Jesus is revealed as Immanuel/God with us, and now he promises that he will be with his followers always (28:20). And his fundamental ministry of saving his people is now passed on to his followers with the goal of salvation from sin (1:21). This task involves reaching out to all nations throughout the world.

The Great Commission is not only for strong, gifted Christians. Chapter 28 stresses the weakness of Jesus' followers. They are apt to doubt (28:17) and yet to worship. Fear and great joy struggle together within them (28:8). It is such ordinary Christians that Jesus commands to go and make disciples of all nations, but he reassures them first that he has all authority, not only in heaven but also here on earth. Therefore they can go with him in full confidence.

Make disciples

The main verb in the Great Commission is to 'make disciples of all nations', with the addition of the participles 'going', 'baptising' and 'teaching'. The fundamental purpose of Jesus is therefore that through the witness of his followers people from all nations might become his disciples. Jesus does not merely want converts, but people who will be disciples and learn from him as their teacher. Mission is not just the gaining of as many 'scalps' as possible, but so preaching the gospel that people begin a new life of wholehearted discipleship. While little newborn babies fascinate us all and we find them beautiful, twenty-year-old babies are a tragedy. Just as babies should develop and grow steadily into maturity, so also newly born-again Christians need to become mature disciples who will learn from Jesus, the great teacher. Christian mission challenges people not just to the initial decision to believe in Jesus' death and resurrection, but to grow as Christian disciples.

This task of making disciples relates to 'all nations', so no church or Christian can be considered faithful to Christ if they do not have a concern for all peoples all over the world. International mission is central to the life of any church or Christian who wants to be faithful to Jesus and to the New Testament.

The word for 'nations' is the usual word which is used for 'Gentiles'. It therefore relates particularly to the fact that the early Jewish church was to evangelise not only its own Jewish people, but also the Gentiles of all nations. The gospel is for all peoples everywhere.

Go

It is commonly noted that in the Old Testament Israel was never sent out into the Gentile world to preach the message of her God. The one exception to that rule remains the prophet Jonah – and he did not much care for his calling to be God's instrument in bringing a message of repentance to Gentile Nineveh. But already in the original call of the disciples they received the mandate to be 'sent out to preach' (Mark 3:14). Now, too, in the final command of the resurrected Jesus they are commanded to 'go', not merely to stay in Israel to demonstrate by their lives the glory and holiness of their God.

Thus the Old Testament call of Israel is supplemented by the New Testament commission. The people of God are not only to live out the holiness of God in their individual and communal lives so that the Gentiles will be attracted in to Zion to worship the God of Israel. The Church is also called to move out into the world to preach the good news of Jesus Christ, his atoning death and life-giving resurrection. As the light of the world the Church has both callings – to live like a magnet which draws people in to the beauty of the Lord, and also to preach the good news beyond the borders of the Church.

Baptising

Baptism as the outward sign of a covenant relationship with God is vitally important. Weak human beings seem to need visible and even tangible signs alongside verbal promises to bolster our faith. For example, in many societies promises of love and marriage are sealed with a ring. So in the biblical covenants God's word of promise is accompanied by visible signs – a rainbow, circumcision or baptism and the Lord's Supper.

Throughout the New Testament verbal witness and visible signs go hand in hand. So in the Great Commission the disciples are commanded not only to go and make disciples, but also to confirm their mission with the visible sign of baptism.

In mission today the outward tokens of the Christian faith carry particular significance. People are drawn to the gospel or alienated from it by the buildings in which we worship. The furnishings and ornamentation of the church also play a vital part. Even ecclesiastical robes, dark suits or casual informal dress convey a message to those who visit a church. As Christians we need to be careful about the external forms which go together with the message we preach and teach.

In many cultures it is baptism which is seen as the crucial event when a person crosses the line from following some other faith into becoming a Christian. I remember an early gathering of converted Muslims in Singapore. Nine of them gathered together, never having met each other before because they belonged to different churches. When they shared their testimonies none of them mentioned their new birth or conversion. But all stressed their baptism, for that was the crux decision for them. No one persecuted them for what they believed in their hearts. But when they got baptised their Muslim society fell on them with fierce opposition. It was their decision concerning baptism which constituted their determination to follow Jesus Christ whatever the cost.

Teaching
Mission circles today often so stress the pioneer church-planting ministry that the teaching and training of national churches is sidelined. Missionary slogans like 'unreached peoples', 'the 10/40 window' or 'adopt a people' have their uses in motivating churches and individual Christians for the task of mission, but they can over-emphasise evangelism to the neglect of other aspects of mission. But in Matthew 28 the task of mission is seen to include making ongoing disciples and then teaching them the fullness of the Christian faith. Jesus evidently wants his people

43

to become mature in their discipleship. As Paul notes in Ephesians 5:25–7, Christ desires to make his Church holy and radiant, 'without stain or wrinkle or any other blemish, but holy and blameless'. Through the taught word of God Christians can so grow in holiness that their witness to the outside world will carry conviction and credibility.

In mission it is our particular aim so to teach and train local Christians that they may be equipped for evangelism, and then also to disciple new believers. In 2 Timothy 2:2 the apostle urges Timothy to teach reliable Christians who will then be able to pass on the teaching to others. Christian mission looks for such a chain reaction. God commands us – we pass on his commands and teach others – they in their turn teach yet others . . .

In our own mission experience we have observed the rightness of this strategy of mission. In Indonesia our mission worked largely within existing Indonesian churches to teach and train them, so that they would be more effective in their ministry. The little group of churches my wife and I worked with in the 1960s was one small example of the wisdom of this policy. Partly as a result of our work in inspiring and teaching, our denomination grew from 20,000 members to 25,000 during the two years we were there. In the following four years they grew to about 80,000 members and continued to grow in the ensuing years.

Recently I was asked whether I would be willing to accept an invitation to preach and teach about mission among Muslims in a group of American churches. They then asked for further information concerning me and the mission work I had been involved in. Their first question was: how many Muslims have you led to Christ? This was followed by the question: how many ex-Muslim churches had I planted? In all honesty I had to reply that I had led very few Muslims to Christ and had not myself planted any churches, but that through my teaching the Indonesian churches had become more effective in their outreach and had planted numerous churches. In fact, our churches grew by some 5,000 members in two years. But the invitation was cancelled as I had not done the evangelism myself.

What a sadly inadequate and unbiblical understanding of Christian mission!

So Christ's final climactic command to his disciples, and thus to us, is to make disciples of all nations. The means is by going rather than staying where we are, by baptising and developing the external forms of the Church. And then, finally, we are told to teach local Christians everything the Lord has taught us. If Christ has commanded us to go out in mission to all nations, then it is our duty to share that command with the churches to which we go. The international mission mandate belongs to all churches and all Christians everywhere. Unless we pass on this mission commission we remain disobedient to these final words of the risen Christ. It is in this context that the title 'Immanuel' has its fulfilment. God in Jesus Christ promises to be with us as we obey his command to make disciples of all nations, Jew and Gentile alike.

3

Luke and the Gentiles

Luke's missionary heart is evident right from the outset of his Gospel. Although he openly acknowledges that other accounts of the life of Jesus had already been written (1:1), he nevertheless felt it right to add his own contribution to these records. He is not only interested in the historical facts, nor just in the theological significance of what he writes. While it remains true that he has 'carefully investigated' the records handed down by 'eyewitnesses and servants of the word', his primary purpose is that Theophilus should gain assured certainty concerning the Christian teaching (1:4). The missionary task of the Church aims to lead believers into an assured certainty of faith.

Whether Theophilus was an actual historical person or just a literary device, Luke's desire is to teach the word of the Lord to such Greek or Roman leaders. It is for this missionary purpose that Luke underlines the fact that Jesus in the Gospel and Paul in Acts adhere obediently to the Law. Leading Romans like Theophilus need not be put off the gospel of Jesus because of any antinomian behaviour. Jesus and his followers are not the ones who have caused the mob disorder which has taken place around them. Luke has an apologetic purpose in his writing. Whereas Mark announces that Jesus is 'the Son of God' immediately in his very first verse, Luke only introduces this controversial and provocative title in 1:32, 35. At the time of the New Testament the Roman emperors had deified their predecessors and thus the emperor would call himself 'son of God'. Luke was surely aware that in referring to Jesus as Son of God he was directly challenging the Roman emperors. He was claiming that Jesus alone is the supreme Son of God. It is surely significant, therefore, that he places this title in the mouth of an angel, giving it divine authority.

The words Luke uses in his introduction reflect the importance of a teaching ministry. The word for 'handed down' (*paredosan*) signifies the whole tradition of Christian faith handed down from former generations. He stresses 'the word' (*logos*) (1:2, 4; cf. John 1:1) and uses the catechetical *katechethes* (1:4; cf. Acts 18:25). As is equally true in the other Gospels, Luke emphasises Jesus' and then the apostles' *words*. Words reveal the truth of God and they are his instruments by which he achieves his purposes. In modern times, words may have become devalued as unreliable political verbiage which masks the truth, but the Gospels stress the central role of words in God's mission. Followers of Jesus, the living Word, are called to become 'servants of the word' (1:2). Verbal witness is central to biblical mission.

While Luke does not quote Old Testament verses as Matthew does in his 'fulfilment verses', he frequently has an underlying Old Testament teaching. This theme is already introduced by the word 'fulfilled' in 1:1. And his use of 'must' (*dei*) implies that the whole history of Jesus takes place in accordance with Old Testament prophecy. *Dei* occurs forty-four times in Luke/Acts and relates to every major event and ministry in the life of Jesus. Jesus, and then his apostles, must submit to the will of the Father which has been laid down in the Old Testament (e.g. 4:43). In his *Themes of St Luke* (Gregorian University Press, 1970) J. Navone says in his exposition of Luke's use of *dei*, 'Jesus himself submits to that will . . . So too do his witnesses.' This is particularly evident when Jesus foretells his coming sufferings and death.

First for the Jew (chapters 1–3)

Luke's first three chapters are very Jewish in character and expression. Elizabeth and Zechariah mirror Hannah and Elkanah with the birth of Samuel. Simeon and Anna in the temple in Jerusalem seem to jump out of the Old Testament as they wait longingly for the coming Messiah. Mary's song reflects that of Hannah, while Zechariah's resonates with Old Testament language – 'the Lord, the God of Israel', 'his servant David', 'our father Abraham', etc. And John the Baptist, with his prophetic ministry in the wilderness, steps right out of the pages of the Old Testament, even quoting Isaiah verbatim (3:4). Luke had evidently learned from his mentor Paul that the gospel is 'first for the Jew' (Rom. 1:16), both time-wise and also in priority. Luke does not, therefore, progress to an emphasis on the Gentiles until after these very Jewish chapters.

But already he hints that mission will go wider, even to the Gentiles of all nations. These first chapters are like an overture in which the main theme of the symphony makes its first appearance. Even Zechariah's song concludes with the fact that God's mercy comes not only 'to us', but also to the Gentiles, those who are 'living in darkness' outside God's covenant with Israel. Simeon rejoices that God's salvation is now for 'all people, a light for revelation to the Gentiles' as well as glory for Israel (2:31–2). God's salvation is indeed for 'all mankind' (3:6). God can move beyond the confines of Israel to raise up children for Abraham (3:8).

Luke's repeated emphasis on the supremacy of the Holy Spirit in Jesus' birth fulfils the Old Testament expectation that the Messiah's coming would be marked by an outpouring of the Holy Spirit with power. This relates particularly to the prophecy of Joel 2:28–9, which starts with the hope that God will pour out his Spirit 'on all people' and promises that 'everyone who calls on the name of the LORD will be saved' (Joel 2:32). The coming of Jesus fulfils all eschatological expectations.

So these chapters already contain the major themes of Luke's

Gospel. Jesus has come to save his people in 'the forgiveness of their sins', for Jesus is the Saviour, 'Christ the Lord' (1:77; 2:11). And 'his people' will now include both Jews and Gentiles. Luke underlines the *mercy* of the Lord in response to faith, with consequent *joy*. Already it becomes clear that God favours the poor and humbles the rich and proud. The key role of Jerusalem and the temple in Luke's writings is also evident in these first chapters. Indeed, the Gospel not only commences in Jerusalem, but will also conclude there (24:52–3). John the Baptist sets the scene for the mission of Jesus' followers in 'preaching a baptism of repentance for the forgiveness of sins' (3:3) and preaching 'the good news' (3:18). And this section ends with Jesus' baptism, when God assures him that he is his beloved Son with whom he is well pleased. The loving relationship of God as Father and Jesus as his beloved Son underlies the whole Gospel. This becomes evident in Jesus' constant life of prayer.

The genealogy

It is commonly noted that Luke's genealogy of Jesus goes right back to Adam, the son of God, while Matthew's stops at Abraham. Clearly Luke is wanting to teach that Jesus as Messiah is not only for Jews, but also for all peoples. Although God's covenant with Abraham promised that he would be the father of 'all peoples on earth' (Gen. 12:3), Abraham was still seen as the father of Israel. Adam, on the other hand, is clearly the progenitor of all peoples. So Luke reminds his readers that God's concern reaches out to all nations.

In passing we have to note that Luke calls Adam 'the son of God'. Our modern mission context of witness among Jews and Muslims compels us to analyse further the title 'son of God', for they both strongly reject the Christian affirmation that Jesus is God's Son. In the Old Testament Adam was God's son because he perfectly mirrored the nature of the Father. Then after the Fall Israel was called to be the children of God. Both Adam and Israel failed to demonstrate the absolute holiness of God in their lives and thus failed to be the image of God, so Jesus came as the unique and perfect divine Son. He is the perfect human and the fulfilment of Israel with the fullness of the godhead dwelling bodily in him (Col. 2:9). When we see Jesus, therefore, we see God. At first the title 'Son of God' was understood as meaning the second Adam, the perfect Israel, and it therefore had merely human significance. Already in New Testament times, however, it seems to have gained its present divine sense.

Matthew placed his genealogy at the outset of his Gospel, but Luke's only appears between the birth narratives and the outset of Jesus' ministry. Going right back to Adam as son of God, the genealogy forms a bridge between the very Jewish chapters and the beginning of Jesus' actual ministry, with its emphasis on the Gentiles. As the introduction to Gentile mission it could not have come at the start of the Gospel, as it does in Matthew.

Jesus begins his ministry (chapter 4)

Jesus must have been so excited when the Holy Spirit descended upon him bodily like a dove and he heard the very voice of the Father assuring him of his love as his beloved Son. But as we have already noted, a spiritual 'high' is often followed by a wilderness experience of temptation. Despite the NIV transla-tion, Jesus was not led 'by' the Spirit. He was full of the Spirit and was 'in' the Spirit as he was led into the wilderness. Luke avoids all suggestion that Jesus was in any way *under* the Spirit, but he knows the power of the Spirit as he faces satanic tempta-tion.

Initially Jesus is tempted to use his miraculous power for selfish purposes in turning a stone into bread. The devil then claimed to have authority over the kingdoms of this world in his hands and offered to pass this glory on to Jesus. The implica-tion is political in character. Unlike Mohammed, who accepted the offer of political power when he moved in the Hijra from Mecca to Medina, Jesus rejects power in favour of the way of the cross. Finally, Satan tempted Jesus to view his calling as God's Son in a wrong way. By the power of the Spirit and the right use of Scripture Jesus defeated Satan. Luke shows that the devil attacks Jesus not only at the outset of his ministry, but also climactically through Judas in his betrayal and death. So Luke adds that Satan left him 'until an opportune time' (4:13). The cross would be the culmination of Satan's attack and his final defeat. The followers of Jesus throughout history have rejoiced that we therefore now face an already defeated foe.

So Jesus went to Galilee in the power of the Spirit. There he taught, Sabbath after Sabbath, in their synagogues, finally returning to Nazareth itself. Here he was invited to chant the Scriptures in the Jewish fashion. The appointed passage came from Isaiah 61, but he stopped halfway through a sentence which must have been electrifying to his audience. He purposely omitted 'the day of God's vengeance' when proclaiming that 'today this scripture is fulfilled'. In Isaiah, God's blessing on Israel includes the prophecy that 'aliens will shepherd your flocks; foreigners will work your fields and vineyards' (Isa. 61:5). But Jesus' kingdom is no longer centred on Israel to the disadvantage of the Gentiles. It is equally for all people of all nations who follow him.

The verses quoted in 4:18–19 have a twofold thrust. They emphasise that the Spirit is on Jesus to anoint him to *preach good news* (literally 'to evangelise'), and twice it is said that he is sent to *proclaim* (literally 'to preach'). Then, too, these verses underline ministry to the poor, prisoners, blind and oppressed, with the equality and justice of the Jubilee year in mind, 'the year of the Lord's favour'. So in these verses Luke combines a social ministry of justice on behalf of the needy and poor with an evangelistic preaching mission. In the practice of Christian mission these two need to be kept together.

People in the synagogue evidently noticed how Jesus avoided negative words about the Gentiles and how he showed real concern for the poor. They therefore 'spoke well of him' and were amazed at his 'words of grace' (4:22, my literal translation).

Isaiah 61 is clearly eschatological in character, and Jesus affirms that 'Today this scripture is fulfilled.' Throughout his writings Luke clearly demonstrates that the coming of Jesus in the power of the Spirit marks the arrival of the end time. This is further highlighted by Luke's repeated use of 'today' and 'now'. The kingdom has indeed come. The history of the Christian Church is lived out in the between-times between Jesus' incarnation and the final fulfilment of the kingdom.

The Nazareth synagogue incident is rightly considered Jesus' manifesto for his life and ministry. The conclusion is that a prophet is often not accepted among his own people in his own country – the NIV misinterprets the word 'country' as 'home town' (cf. 15:13, 15; 19:12). These words foreshadow Israel's rejection of Jesus and the opening of the door for Gentiles. So Jesus goes on to scandalise his hearers by reminding them how the prophets Elijah and Elisha ministered also to Gentiles. In traditional Jewish thought, the kingdom was expected to relate to all nations. Universality is the hallmark of the kingdom and also of Jesus' ministry. The history of the Christian Church is therefore the history of how the gospel reaches out to all peoples everywhere. Again we note that international mission is a core value for Christians.

The inauguration of the kingdom in the ministry of Jesus is marked by his power over evil spirits (4:31–7, 41), his healing of the sick (4:38–40; 5:12–26), his preaching the good news of the kingdom (4:43–4), his power over nature (5:1–11) and his calling of disciples to follow him (5:10–11, 27–31; 6:12–16).

Already in 5:10 Jesus foresees that Peter, as indeed all his disciples, would follow him in becoming 'fishers of men and women'. The ministry of the kingdom is begun by Jesus, but must be carried on by his Church throughout the ages. Luke develops this theme in the continuation of Jesus' ministry through his apostles in the book of Acts.

It should be noted that Jesus spent a whole night in prayer with his Father before calling the Twelve. Luke observes how Jesus consistently spends considerable time alone in prayer before every important event in his life. And his natural tendency, even in the agony of the cross, is to turn to his Father in prayer.

Jesus and prayer

In Luke's Gospel Jesus not only demonstrates in his life the central role of prayer, but also teaches it by word. Luke records nine specific prayers of Jesus and two parables on prayer.

Jesus' life of prayer moved his disciples to long for such relationship with the Father in their own lives. They therefore asked Jesus to teach them to pray (11:1) – not just *how* to pray. This fundamental request led to Jesus giving them the model prayer, the so-called Lord's Prayer. The contrast between the initial 'your' and the ensuing 'our' is striking. In prayer the primary aim is the honour of the Lord's name and the coming of his kingdom. This dual purpose places the prayer firmly in the context of our mission calling, in which the primary motive is the glory of the Lord and the building of his kingdom.

Luke places this passage on prayer immediately after Jesus' encounter with Martha and Mary (10:38–42) in which he praises Mary for her quiet 'listening to what he said'. In contrast, Martha was anxiously busy and allowed this to distract her from being with Jesus, which was much more important. Worldly anxiety easily prevents true discipleship with its more permanent values (cf. 8:14; 12:13–34; 21:34). Likewise, prayer and the call to mission may be drowned by such materialistic concerns.

Jesus' parable concerning the friend asking for bread at midnight surely made his audience smile. In societies without electricity and where people sleep where they drop, it is difficult to get up in the night – you can easily step on the body of a sleeping child or relative, with disastrous consequences! As missionaries in Indonesia in the early 1960s we learned this by never-to-be-forgotten experience! So the householder wisely pretended not to hear his friend's call. But because of his 'boldness' the friend got up and gave the required bread. The word really means 'importunate solicitation', 'pertinacious importunity' – or, in common English, the friend made a fearful nuisance of himself! Using continuous present tenses Jesus then teaches that we should ask and go on asking, knock and go on knocking, seek and go on seeking. Persistent prayer is highlighted also in 18:1–8. Such prayer will yield fruit. Our Father delights to give his children good gifts and will particularly bestow his Holy Spirit on those who go on asking him. So, in the generous grace of God, prayer and the Holy Spirit of mission go hand in hand together.

Sadly, the disciples were slow to realise the vital importance of prayer when Jesus called them to pray with him in Gethsemane. He warned them that prayer was needed if they were not to fall into temptation (22:40, 46), but they slept – and in the time of trial they forsook him and fled (Mark 14:50). Three men failed to pray and the whole body of Jesus' disciples failed – is this a lesson for the Church today?

Salvation

Of the synoptics, Luke alone calls Jesus 'Saviour' (2:11), although he is not alone in underlining the fact that Jesus saves (e.g. Matt. 1:21). Four times in Luke Jesus says 'your faith has saved you'. He affirms that he has come to 'seek and to save what was lost' (19:10), to call 'sinners to repentance', for it is not the healthy or the righteous who need a doctor (5:31, 32).

In Chapter 15 Jesus tells three parables in response to the Pharisees' complaint that he welcomed and ate with sinners (15:2). In each of these parables of the Lost Sheep, the Lost Coin and the Lost Son, the emphasis is on 'find' and 'rejoice'. Even in the second half of the parable of the Lost Son the story climaxes in the act of 'celebrating and being glad'. The lost has been found, the dead has returned to life. The fitting response is 'music and dancing' with the 'fattened calf'. Mission and celebrating go together!

Commentators suggest that the older brother represents the leaders of Israel, while the prodigal's return foreshadows the coming of sinners and Gentiles to Jesus. The father's longing for his son's return, and the eager searching of the shepherd for the lost sheep and the woman for her coin, reflect God's longing for sinners to repent and turn to him. Likewise, Jesus willingly goes even to the cross to bring the lost to new life. These parables challenge the Christian Church to sacrificial service in order to seek the lost, even, if necessary, neglecting 'the righteous' to give priority to our evangelistic outreach. They also remind us to rejoice and celebrate with great joy when sinners turn to Jesus Christ and find new life. In this we share with the angels in heaven and with God himself.

In his Gospel Luke repeatedly notes the importance of repentance and 'turning' to Jesus as the prerequisites for life in the kingdom of God. Such repentance is the human response with faith to the grace and mercy of God. The order is clear: grace – repentance and turning – God's mercy extended – salvation through the cross and resurrection. Salvation then leads on to following Jesus, praising God and telling others the good news of salvation (e.g. 8:47; 18:43).

But Luke's use of the words 'save' and 'salvation' have wide significance. Related words are used in the contexts of healing from sickness, deliverance from evil spirits and from a storm, even salvation from enemies (1:74), but the foundation for all aspects of salvation lies in the forgiveness of sin. As in all the Gospels, therefore, the goal of the whole life of Jesus is in his death on the cross and his resurrection. Everything in the life and ministry of Jesus leads towards the cross. Through his cross and resurrection salvation comes to sinners. The book of Acts will show how the apostles therefore preached a message of the cross and resurrection. This lies at the heart not only of evangelistic preaching, but also of all Christian teaching and discipling of believers. As Christians we need constantly to challenge ourselves to check whether this is actually the case in our ministry.

In his saving work Jesus particularly relates to the poor and oppressed. In the 'Sermon on the Plain', Luke omits Matthew's 'in spirit' when Jesus declares blessing on the poor (6:20, cf. Matt. 5:3), and likewise God's favour rests on those who 'hunger now' without Matthew's added 'for righteousness'. The poor tend to become the oppressed, those who lack status and position in society. Other people will hardly bother to deliver them from their lowly position and they lack the resources to deliver themselves. So the poor are those who look in humility to God for his salvation. On the other hand, the rich tend to trust in themselves and their own wealth for life's satisfaction. Their heart is fixed on money and position, so it is hard for them to turn to Jesus and follow him in poverty. No wonder Jesus declares that it is 'easier for a camel to go through the eye of a needle than for a rich man to enter the kingdom of God' (18:25). His hearers realised that he was talking of salvation and his words elicited the response, 'Who then can be saved?'

Jesus' story of the rich man and Lazarus (18:19–31) declares that the rich man has his reward here and now on earth, so he has no reward stored up for him in eternity. He is dressed in imperial purple (rabbinic tradition maintained that God is dressed in purple) while Lazarus has nothing except sores and hunger. The rich man asks that Lazarus be sent to his five brothers to warn them of impending judgment and bring them to repentance, but he is told that Moses and the Prophets suffice. So the unrepentant rich suffer the agonies of hell, while Lazarus is comforted in the presence of Abraham himself.

Luke assumes not only that wealth means people concentrating their thoughts on material things to the neglect of God and his righteousness, but also that wealth is often ill-gotten. Repentance and following Jesus must therefore mean giving one's wealth to the poor or to those whom one has deceived. As Jesus' disciple one needs to give ill-gotten wealth away and follow him in poverty. It is when Zacchaeus gives generously to the poor and returns the money he has gained by cheating that Jesus declares, 'Today salvation has come to this house' (19:9). Because the disciples gave up everything to follow Jesus they can rest assured of eternal life (18:29, 30).

The new exodus

Commentators agree that Luke 9:51 marks a new direction in Luke's Gospel. Jesus 'sets out for Jerusalem'. He now walks in the footsteps of Israel in the exodus from Egypt and the journey to the promised land. Jesus heads for Jerusalem, where he will re-enact the Passover in his own sacrificial death for the salvation of his people.

Luke 9 introduces this new departure with the Transfiguration (9:28–36) where the glory of Jesus is made manifest, while at the same time Moses and Elijah (representing the Law and the Prophets) spoke of his 'departure'/exodus. The glory of the Lord is inseparable from his impending suffering. The heavenly voice which had spoken at his baptism now repeats, 'This is my Son, whom I have chosen,' but adds the urgent 'Listen to him.' Luke does not hesitate to show how the disciples failed to obey that word. They lacked the faith to deal with a demon-possessed child (9:40) and they quarrelled among themselves over which of them was the greatest (9:46). How incongruous, when Jesus had just stated with deep urgency (9:44) that he would suffer at his enemies' hands!

The exodus theme draws towards its final climax with Jesus' entry into Jerusalem (19:28–44). In fulfilment of prophecy he does not come in military splendour on a horse, but meekly on a donkey. By repetition Luke underlines the question 'Why?' and the appropriate answer 'The Lord needs it.' The question 'Why?' often surfaces in times of suffering and humiliation, but the answer must always centre on the will of God rather than on our own desires or comfort.

Although Jesus was received with popular acclaim as 'the king who comes in the name of the Lord', he knew that Jerusalem's ultimate rejection of him as Messiah would lead to the destruction of the city and the temple (19:41–4). Jesus then proceeded to show that, sadly, the temple had ceased to be a holy place, for people had turned it into 'a den of robbers' which needed the Messiah's cleansing. With the coming cross and resurrection,

Jerusalem and the temple as the locus of God's presence and the place of sacrifice would become redundant, for their fulfilment in Jesus himself had come. Their destruction by the Romans was timely.

The new section of the Gospel beginning with 9:51 immediately takes the ministry of Jesus beyond the confines of the people of Israel. Against normal Jewish practice at that time, Jesus went through Samaria on his way from Galilee to Jerusalem. The Samaritans were the product of mixed Jew–Gentile marriages and followed a form of religion which included both Jewish and alien elements. They accepted the Pentateuch but rejected the rest of the Old Testament. They sacrificed in a temple, but not the Jerusalem temple. The Samaritans formed a bridge between Jews and Gentiles. So Luke stresses Jesus' ministry to Samaritans. Thus ten lepers are healed, but only the one who was a Samaritan returns to give thanks (17:11–19). And in chapter 10 it is the Samaritan, not the Jewish leaders, who exemplifies love for neighbour.

In 9:1 Jesus called the twelve and sent them out in mission with his power and authority. The number twelve in Jewish thought stands for the people of Israel because of the twelve tribes. For this reason Jesus called to himself twelve disciples, for they were the fulfilment of the people of Israel. Then, in 10:1, Jesus appointed seventy or seventy-two others and sent them out. Jewish traditional thought had considered seventy to be the number of the Gentiles, following the number of the sons of Noah in Genesis 10. But around the first century debate raged as to whether seventy-two might not be the right number for the Gentiles. This debate may also be seen with reference to the Septuagint, the Greek and therefore Gentile translation of the Hebrew Scriptures. It had been called 'Septuagint' because it was translated by seventy elders. But around the first century it became normal to say it was translated by seventy-two elders. The mathematical number was not as important as its significance. So in Luke 10:1 the seventy or seventy-two would seem clearly to signify Gentile mission.

We note that Jesus did not replace the Twelve with the seventy, but rather added the seventy 'others' also. Gentile mission does not replace Jewish mission, but is added to it. The Jewish foundation of the Church remains, but Gentiles are added to the Jewish stock.

In Acts we shall again have reason to note the development of mission from Jews through Samaritans also to Gentiles. Luke underlines the opposition which the Church would face in moving beyond the confines of Israel, by placing 9:57–62 between Jesus' venture to the Samaritans and his call of the seventy/seventy-two. Gentile mission would call for sacrificial commitment.

Luke's particular concern for the Gentiles has led some critics to declare that he was a Gentile. But Luke's constant use of Hebraisms would seem to deny this. And Luke still emphasises the validity of Paul's 'to the Jew first'. Indeed the evidence seems to suggest that Luke was a Jew like all the other New Testament writers. But he was a Hellenistic Jew, and through his work with Paul (see the 'we' passages in Acts) he had gained a special interest in mission to the Gentiles. Like Paul, his concern for the Gentiles did not, however, preclude a love for his own Jewish people.

The banquet

The telephone rang and a politely sophisticated voice announced that it was the BBC. They had been informed that I was an expert on religion and food! Could they do an interview with me? Over the phone they wanted some indications of my thoughts on this topic. My mind raced and I thought of the Passover meal, Old Testament sacrifices which included communal feasting, Jesus eating with various people, the Lord's Supper which was originally within a meal together, the final messianic banquet. I realised how central to Scripture eating together is. It occurred to me that systematic theology should really have a section on food and eating. This would relate well to Jewish and Middle Eastern cultures, as also to most non-

European societies. Food is culturally very important, and eating together is deeply significant. Luke shares this particular interest.

Luke notes how Jesus purposely ate not only with Pharisees (e.g. 7:36; 14:1), but also with tax collectors and sinners (5:29, 30; 7:33–4; 15:2; 19:7). He encouraged his disciples to invite 'the poor, the crippled, the lame, the blind' (14:13, 21), not those who could repay hospitality.

The supreme act of eating and drinking together is the Lord's Supper (22:7ff.) which Jesus calls 'this Passover'. The Lord's Supper looks back to its roots in the Passover meal, with all the symbolism of liberation from slavery in Egypt and from the angel of death through shed blood. But now Jesus sees the bread and wine representing his own body and blood sacrificed for our salvation and deliverance from the slavery of sin. The Lord's Supper also looks forward to the final consummation of the kingdom in the messianic banquet at the table of Abraham. Jews picture heaven as a great feast, with the Messiah as host and in the presence of Abraham. In the Lord's Supper we therefore feast at that heavenly meal, rejoicing in the presence of the Messiah himself. It is sad that in most modern churches the Communion Service has lost the sense of exultant rejoicing and feasting – a sip of wine and a crumb of bread can hardly be called a feast! And humourless solemnity has replaced the joy of a communal feast. In cross-cultural mission we need to rethink the style of such services/celebrations, particularly in societies where eating and drinking carry considerable significance.

Luke particularly looks forward to the future messianic banquet (e.g. 13:29; 14:15; 22:16, 30). As we have already seen in Matthew, in the miraculous feeding of the five thousand Jesus evidently had the Passover meal and Lord's Supper in mind. So 9:16 uses the appropriate verbs – Jesus 'took' the bread and fish, 'looked up to heaven', 'gave thanks', 'broke them' and 'gave'. In feeding the crowd Jesus foreshadows not only his gift of salvation through his cross, but beyond to the final banquet in glory. Jesus is indeed the Messiah who feeds his people with an abundant feast. And Luke underlines the abundance by placing the event in Bethsaida, 'house of satisfaction'. He then concludes the feeding of the crowd with the statement that they were 'satisfied'.

The sequel to Jesus being called a glutton and drunkard because he 'came eating and drinking' (7:34) is that 'wisdom is proved right by all her children'. We have already observed that Jesus eats not only with the rich, but particularly with the poor and sick. In 7:35 his eating is in an even wider context of 'all', implying those from every background, every nation and every people. Rich and poor, Jews and Gentiles, are included in the banquet. The guests who were first invited to the wedding feast refused the offer. Now all sorts of despised people sit at the master's banquet to 'feast in the kingdom of God' (14:15–24).

In the final resurrection appearance Jesus demonstrated his bodily reality by eating fish with his disciples (24:40–3). This is immediately followed by the Lukan 'Great Commission' when Jesus declared that his death and resurrection with the call to repentance unto the forgiveness of sins will be declared to all nations. The disciples are then commissioned to be 'witnesses of these things' (24:48). The joys of fellowship in eating with Jesus will lead to mission witness and preaching the good news of salvation in Jesus the Messiah.

Luke 24:45–9 declares the heart of the Christian message. As will become abundantly clear in Acts, Jesus' death and resurrection form the foundation of the good news. God's purpose for the Church is to preach this message to all nations. In so doing we look for a response of repentance, knowing that God will give his forgiveness to those who turn in faith to the Lord. For this task we need the power of the Holy Spirit (24:49). These are Jesus' final conclusive words to his people before he ascends back to his Father. A church or Christian who ignores this mission command is radically disobedient to the Lord. But we need not fear, for he gives us the enabling power of his Spirit as we go out in obedience to his call.

4

The gospel spreads
(Acts of the Apostles)

What a blockbuster! Hollywood would be hard put to rival the drama and excitement of the book of Acts. Tongues of fire and consequent accusations of drunkenness – God judges Ananias and Sapphira and they drop dead – apostles imprisoned, flogged, stoned to death – divine earthquake allows apostles to escape prison mob demonstrations and lynchings – storm at sea and shipwreck – apostle bitten by snake – fearless bold preaching – mass movements to Christ – the extensive spread of the gospel round the Mediterranean and out to Gentiles as well as Jews. What a story! But Luke is not only writing to entertain or even to give accurate history. He wants his readers to learn that his Gospel's account of Jesus is not complete with the cross and resurrection. Jesus is still active by his Spirit, and his purposes for Jews and Gentiles unfold.

While the Gospel declares what 'Jesus began to do and to teach' (Acts 1:1), in Acts Jesus works by his Spirit in and through the apostles and early Church. The miracles the apostles perform in Jesus' name parallel those done by Jesus in the Gospel. Likewise, the early Church enjoyed 'the favour of all the people' (2:47), reminding us of Jesus' growth (Luke 2:52).

It is Jesus who instructs the apostles to remain in Jerusalem until they receive the gift of the Holy Spirit. The Jesus who would ascend 'into heaven' (1:11) promises to come 'from heaven' by his Spirit (2:2). And it is to Jesus that they turn with their questions – would he now 'restore the kingdom to Israel' (1:6)? How sad that at such a crucial time the apostles descended into vain theological speculation concerning politics, times and the fulfilment of prophecy concerning the land of Israel. Such mysteries remain in the Father's hands, not ours. But the devil loves to side-track God's people with such idle debates, so preventing them from concentrating on the more vital calling to mission in the name of Jesus Christ.

The risen Jesus brings them back to his primary purpose. Acts 1:8 features as the foundational text, which Luke then expounds. Acts shows Jesus at work in power by his Spirit through the early Church. And the power of the Spirit is inseparably linked to witness not only in Jerusalem, but even 'to the ends of the earth'. 'You will receive power . . . *and* you will be my witnesses . . .' The interconnecting 'and' is vitally import-ant. We dare not separate the power of Jesus' Spirit from the missionary call to witness worldwide. Sadly, there are some Christians and churches which richly enjoy the power of the Spirit, with all his miraculous gifts and workings, but have no passion for worldwide mission. This failure leads to an ingrown spiritual selfishness. There are equally some who have a deep concern for mission worldwide, but are frightened of the power of the Holy Spirit because they associate this with an extreme charismatic theology which they do not accept. But without the power of the Spirit all mission will be fruitless and frustrating. We need the power of the Spirit *and* passionate involvement in international mission.

Holy Spirit power

Repeatedly throughout Acts, the distinguishing mark and consequence of God's acceptance is the gift of the Holy Spirit. When the Jerusalem Christians doubt whether it is right to accept Samaritans or Gentiles as Christians, they are convinced by the fact that they too received the Holy Spirit just as the first Christians had received him. The evidence was often manifest through the ecstatic gifts of tongues and prophecy. At such controversial turning points in the development of the Christian Church, God delighted to pour out these spectacular gifts of power.

At Pentecost, too, the initial outpouring of the Holy Spirit on the first Jewish and God-fearing Christians was accompanied by an audible 'violent wind' and visible 'tongues of fire'. The Christians then spoke 'in other tongues' so that Jewish pilgrims from many places heard God's word in their own languages.

Throughout Acts the Holy Spirit performs mighty 'signs and wonders' – an expression which comes nine times in Acts. The word 'signs' shows the purpose of the miraculous 'wonders'. The Spirit heals miraculously, delivers people from demons, raises the dead, breaks open prisons to free his apostles, gives visions and dreams, negates a viper's poison, etc. No open-minded reader of Acts can fail to appreciate the reality of the Spirit's power.

Judgment

This power is also manifest in judgment as people sin against the holiness and sovereign glory of God. So, in Acts 5, Ananias and Sapphira lie against the Holy Spirit in saying falsely that they had sold all their land and were giving all the proceeds to God's Church. When they fell down dead at Peter's feet, their divine judgment made everyone realise the power of the Holy Spirit and the dreadful seriousness of sin. As a result, 'great fear seized the whole church and all who heard about these events' (5:11). This leads on naturally in the next verse to the general statement that 'the apostles performed many miraculous signs and wonders among the people' – no wonder the Church grew massively!

Again in Acts 12, Herod's arrogant pride is manifest as he sits publicly upon his throne in royal robes receiving the acclamation of the crowds. 'This is the voice of a god, not of a man,' they cried (12:22). Because he evidently received this flattering praise with pleasure, without acknowledging that God is to be praised, an angel struck him down 'and he was eaten by worms and died'. In such a context it is hardly surprising that the next verse declares, 'The word of God continued to increase and spread.'

In Acts 13, Elymas the sorcerer opposed the apostles and tried to prevent the proconsul Sergius Paulus from believing. Paul's words of condemnation (13:10) may sound excessive to mild-mouthed Europeans, but we should not impose our cultural patterns of speech on others. And God supported Paul's words and struck Elymas blind. Once again the miraculous working of the Holy Spirit in judgment brought fruit. When the proconsul 'saw what had happened, he believed, for he was amazed at the teaching about the Lord'. So it was not only the miraculous sign which led him to faith, but also the teaching of the apostle. Sign and word go hand in hand in mission.

Power for holy living

The early chapters of Acts give a vivid description of the early Church in its life together. This was a community which experienced miraculous signs and wonders alongside its bold preaching and witness. This is exemplified in the healing of the crippled beggar (3:1–10), but evidently multitudes of sick and demon-possessed people found healing in the name of Jesus (5:12–16). The early Christians were a people of powerful prayer (4:31) which resulted in their meeting place being shaken. All of them were again filled with the Spirit, with the consequence that they 'spoke the word of God boldly' (4:31).

Chapter 2 verse 42 summarises the close fellowship of these first Christians. They 'devoted themselves to the apostles' teaching', to *koinonia* fellowship together, to the deeply symbolic act of sharing food together and to prayer. This fellowship was expressed in sharing everything they had. So the Christians 'were one in heart and mind' (4:32).

We may note that fellowship is not only in praying and eating together, but also in the mutual sharing of possessions. In this way fellowship removed all inequalities and the Church became a model of real justice. Is the word 'fellowship', therefore, the New Testament equivalent to the Old Testament 'justice'? In his Gospel Luke shows particular concern for the social dimension of mission in bringing good news to the poor and needy, so it may be expected that in Acts, too, caring for the poor will stand out as a major characteristic of the Church. Moral righteousness in the early Church goes together with a shared life of fellowship/justice. Even the widows are cared for. At one stage there seems to have been some discrimination in Jerusalem against 'Grecian' or Hellenistic widows (6:1), but this was quickly put right. True fellowship broke down the barriers between Grecian and Hebraic Jews. Later, too, Paul organises a collection from diaspora churches with largely Gentile membership and sends this to the Hebraic church in Jerusalem. This may have been for practical purposes in a time of famine and it may also have been a conscious fulfilment of Old Testament prophecy (Isa. 60:5), but it doubtless also reinforced the unity of the churches.

As Christian mission leads to the formation of new churches and fellowships, our preaching and praying need to keep the life of the early Church in mind. It is the work of the Holy Spirit to inspire holiness of living in the Church. And the work of the Holy Spirit of Christ in the life and worship of the Church attracts outsiders. The love of Christ manifest in our relationships together in the Church and the pure holiness of our lives will draw non-Christians to faith in Christ.

Luke also particularly stresses the place of women in the early Church, although at that time in ordinary Jewish society women were rather looked down upon. Luke frequently underlines the fact that women were present alongside the men, and he names Rhoda, Dorcas, Lydia and Damaris as well as Mary the mother of Jesus and Mary the mother of John Mark. In 17:12 Luke notes the conversion of various 'prominent Greek women' before going on to say that some Greek men also believed. Likewise, Priscilla's name comes before that of her husband, Aquila (18:18, 26). Negatively, Sapphira played a significant role in her and her husband's sin. Felix' wife Drusilla also merits a mention by name. Luke's positive emphasis on the role of women despite his chauvinistic context is surely significant for the role of women in mission and the Church today. Traditional churches and missions need to rethink their male dominance and their neglect of women's gifts.

'You will be my witnesses' (1:8)

The power of the Holy Spirit giving miraculous signs and holy living in the Church must lead to active witness by word and deed. This witness started in Jerusalem among Jewish people, but spread through Judea and Samaria to the ends of the earth. In so doing, the gospel reached out to Samaritans and then to Gentiles of all races everywhere. So Holy Spirit power and mission must go inseparably together.

Geographically Luke concentrates considerably on the central role of Jerusalem. Not only do the apostles constantly refer back to the authority of the Jerusalem church leaders, but the outreach of the gospel starts there too. So the first chapters of Acts concentrate on the growth of the Church in Jerusalem; but following Jesus' prophetic word the horizons then widen. At first it is only as far as Judea. Then in Acts 8 persecution rages after the martyrdom of Stephen and the Christians scatter to Samaria, with the result that their witness produces a mass movement of Samaritans to Christ. After the conversion of Paul, mission extends around the northern shores of the Mediterranean and finally reaches to Rome, the heart of the Roman empire. The implication of Acts' inconclusive final chapter is that the Church's witness must and will develop further until all the world hears the good news of Jesus.

Ethnically, too, Luke was recording the extension of Christian mission, first among Jewish people and then more widely to Gentiles. Located in Jerusalem and Judea, the first seven chapters of Acts describe the large-scale spread of the gospel among Jews and God-fearers or proselytes. Although the latter were ethnically Gentile, they had joined themselves to the people of Israel in submission to the Jewish Law. Even Pentecost, with its apparent reversal of the scattering of the nations at Babel (Genesis 11), was exclusively experienced by Jews and Gentile adherents to the people of Israel. They came from many parts of the Roman empire and spoke a multitude of languages, but they represented only the Jewish diaspora. So the mission of the Church is 'to the Jew first' (Rom. 1:16, RSV). The primacy of Jewish mission is probably not only temporal, with witness to Jews preceding Gentile mission in the history of the New Testament. It may well also signify God's particular concern for his Jewish people and his heartfelt longing that they too should find life through Jesus as their Messiah. Still today, Jewish evangelism must hold a special place in Christians' mission emphasis.

Although some Gentiles had joined themselves to Israel in the Old Testament, the people of Israel continued to be the one people of God. And religious prejudice against Gentiles remained strong in Israel. This may have been exacerbated in New Testament times by the Jews' bitter war with Rome, and climactically by the destruction of Jerusalem by the Gentile Romans. It cannot, therefore, have been easy for the Jewish apostles to start evangelism among Gentiles. And the early Jewish Church was evidently very uncertain whether it was right to accept Gentiles without them abandoning their foreign ways and becoming part of Israel as Christian God-fearers or proselytes. Hence the question arose as to whether Gentile converts needed to be circumcised and follow the Law. This was to become the pressing issue at the first church consultation in Jerusalem (Acts 15).

In his grace the Lord therefore gave the Church two inter-mediate bridges between Jews and Gentiles to prepare the way for wider mission among all peoples. In Acts 8, Christians flee from persecution to Samaria. As we have seen, the Samaritans stemmed from mixed marriages between Jews and Gentiles and formed a halfway house between Jews and Gentiles.

Jesus had prepared his disciples for a positive approach to Samaritans by his teaching concerning the Good Samaritan. Likewise he healed ten lepers, and the Gospels note that it was only the Samaritan man who returned to say thank you. Jesus also interacted very personally with the Samaritan woman (John 4), with the result that many Samaritans believed. He then purposely went through Samaritan villages en route to Jerusalem (Luke 9:51–6). And in Acts 7:16 Stephen underlines that Jacob was buried in the Samaritan Shechem in the tomb which Abraham had bought.

With this preparation for mission to the Samaritans, the Christians needed no special guidance or vision before they began preaching to Samaritans. They needed no special call. They just went down to Samaria and preached Christ there. When the overall mission purpose of God is biblically clear, Jesus' followers should not wait for new guidance or a special call. We have only to obey.

The second bridge to Gentile mission is the conversion of the Ethiopian eunuch. He was evidently a Gentile, but he was worshipping in the Jewish temple, reading the Hebrew Scriptures and worshipping the God of Israel. Legally he could not have been a proselyte as a eunuch, but he was a God-fearer. He too prepares the way for wider mission among Gentiles.

The eunuch's question, 'How can I . . . unless someone explains it to me?' (8:31) has major implications for mission practice. Philip had asked him whether he understood the Isaiah passage he was reading. Faceless distribution of Scripture or other Christian literature without some personal relationship can only have limited results.

Philip expounded the passage from Isaiah and told the

Ethiopian about the good news of Jesus (8:35), with the result that he believed and was baptised. This is followed directly by the first account of Paul's conversion. This event is so tremendously important for the history of the Church and its mission that we have three separate accounts of it in Acts (chapters 9, 22 and 26). From the outset of his Christian life, Paul is called to reach out to Gentiles. Nevertheless he starts with Jews only, preaching boldly in the name of Jesus (9:28, 29).

As so often, it is Peter who initiates new movements in the Church. He is the rock on which the Church is established. So it is through Peter that the Roman centurion Cornelius and his household are converted. Luke dedicates almost two whole chapters to this crucial turning point in Christian mission, when the gospel starts to reach out to the Gentile world.

For the Jewish Peter it was not easy to break the Law and consort with Gentiles. He was evidently not rigidly following the Law, for he was staying in the house of a tanner. Dealing with dead bodies made a person ritually unclean, and to stay in a tanner's house goes against rabbinic law. Nevertheless, Peter needed the mind-blowing vision in which he was commanded to kill and eat all sorts of unclean animals – perhaps rats, worms, shellfish, pigs, etc. He needed to learn that he must not call anything unclean which God has cleansed. Only then would he be willing to receive Cornelius' Gentile messengers and go to Cornelius' house to preach.

Luke does not hesitate to note the positive value in God's sight of Cornelius' prayerful and generous godliness before his conversion (10:2). The followers of non-Christian religions may also demonstrate positive goodness and spirituality. God rejoices in all that is good and true. But this godly background does not mean that Cornelius does not need to believe in Jesus Christ and receive forgiveness of sins (10:43). So when Cornelius believed, God bestowed on him the gift of the Holy Spirit to show that Gentiles too are accepted.

After the conversion of Cornelius, Luke notes that most Christians still only preached to Jews, but some 'began to speak to Greeks also' (11:20). The church in Jerusalem evidently had some uncertainty about the widening of mission to include Gentiles, so they sent Barnabas to investigate. When he saw 'the evidence of the grace of God' he rejoiced and the Church grew tremendously (11:22–4).

Gentile witness

In chapter 13 Peter gives way to Paul, the apostle to the Gentiles. Barnabas and Paul are set apart by the church leaders in Antioch for the Lord's work. These prophets and teachers were a very diverse group, including the black-skinned Simeon and the North African Lucius. So they were perhaps ideally suited to receive the Spirit's commission to separate Barnabas and Paul for wider mission.

At this stage Barnabas is named before Paul, and he was evidently the senior partner. Was this why they started their mission in Cyprus, Barnabas' home island? Perhaps it is good to start one's mission work in situations where one feels at home and knows the people. Then one may branch out into wider mission.

But by the time they reach Pisidian Antioch, Paul has taken the lead. At first he preached in the synagogue, appealing to Jews and Gentile God-fearers to receive the message of forgiveness of sins and justification through Jesus (13:38, 39). Many believed and urged Paul to preach again the following Sabbath.

All seemed to be progressing well. The next Sabbath 'almost the whole city gathered to hear the word of the Lord', but the crowd must have included many Gentiles and this angered the Jews. Jealously they abused Paul and Barnabas. Paul and Barnabas reacted with bold words, declaring that the gospel had to be preached first to Jews but they were showing themselves un-worthy of eternal life. Then come the key words which would change the face of Christian and indeed of world history – 'we now turn to the Gentiles' (13:46) – and they quote Isaiah 49:6 as justification for this vital change. From now on, Paul's calling to be the apostle to the Gentiles was paramount in his mind.

Although the Gentiles rejoiced, many Jews reacted with anger and chased the apostles out of the city. It is noteworthy that when they reached Iconium they immediately went first to the synagogue to preach to Jews as well as Gentile God-fearers. Turning to the Gentiles did not mean that the apostles no longer preached to Jews. The gospel of Jesus is for all peoples, both Jews and Gentiles.

There remains some debate concerning the Jewish background to the Church. Does the Church progress in a direct line from its roots in the Old Testament and Jewish faith? Or is the Church a totally new people of God, into which both Jews and Gentiles enter by faith in Jesus? What, therefore, is the position with regard to Jews? As we shall see, Romans 11 clearly indicates the former. God does not plant a new olive tree, but grafts new Gentile branches into the tree of Israel. So although Paul was not bound by rabbinic law, he continued to relate to the synagogue and observe Jewish ritual practices like circumcision (16:3), a vow to cut off his hair (18:18) and the purification rite in which heads were shaved (21:23–4). Evidently Paul's Christian faith did not preclude adherence to the Jewish faith and practices.

Luke particularly emphasises that the apostles did nothing to provoke the fierce opposition of the Jewish crowds or of the Roman authorities. In his declaration of the Christian faith for the sake of Theophilus and other Roman dignitaries, he wants to show that the Christians were innocent of all reprehensible behaviour. All mob violence and social disorder was due to their enemies.

Cross-cultural witness

All the apostolic sermons in Acts are given to Jewish audiences except those to the Lycaonians (14:8–18) and in Athens (17:16–34). In these, the apostles addressed Gentiles who had no background knowledge of the Jewish faith through involvement in the synagogue. Christians today who work among ethnic minorities or who go overseas in cross-cultural mission will share a real fellow-feeling with Paul as apostle to those with no biblical background.

Paul was highly educated and had studied Greek philosophy, so he could use his knowledge to relate the gospel to his Greek audience. In his sermon in Athens he uses the ideas of Greek philosophical schools and quotes a Greek poet to assist his communication. In this way he creates a bridge into the thinking of his audience. Indeed, his whole address is based on his observation that the Athenians were worshipping an unknown god. So he affirms that the Christian God is actually the one whom they worship as unknown – the unknown has become knowable through Jesus Christ. Thus Paul gives us a model for our cross-cultural mission today. Mission workers need to be so trained that they have a good working knowledge of the faiths and philosophies with which they will be working. And then they need to learn to use that knowledge in making the gospel relevant to the prevalent thinking and belief systems.

Both in Lystra and Athens, the fact of creation forms a central element in the apostolic message. With a Jewish audience this was unnecessary, for they knew that God has created all things and all people. In Lystra the apostles urgently appeal to the people not to worship created idols any more, but to turn to the living God who made all things (14:15). God does not need to be 'served by human hands' and he 'does not live in temples built by hands' (17:24–5).

When working as a missionary with the Karo Batak church in Sumatra, Indonesia, I had to learn this biblical principle. I soon noticed that Indonesian Christians always started with the fact of creation when addressing people of traditional religious background. Local people still worshipped the spirits of the local volcanoes and other geographical phenomena, but Christians proclaimed the supremacy of the God who had made all things. In following the Indonesian Christians' example I had to over-come the prejudice of my own background. In England, preaching God as creator led to fierce arguments about evolution, so it sidetracked people from hearing the message of Christ. But in Sumatra at that time we were not faced with that particular problem.

Throughout Acts, and particularly in the sermon in Athens, the resurrection of Jesus lies at the heart of the apostolic message. Also, at his trial before the Sanhedrin Paul declares his faith in the resurrection (23:6). Perhaps as Christians we have sometimes overemphasised the saving work of Christ on the cross to the neglect of the message of new life in the resurrection. Of course, the resurrection cannot be separated from the cross, but nevertheless Paul's emphasis was on the life-giving power of God in raising Jesus from the dead.

It would seem, however, that despite all Paul's careful efforts to relate relevantly to his Gentile audience he failed to communicate what he meant by the resurrection. The Athenians thought he was 'advocating foreign gods' (17:18), namely 'Jesus' and 'Resurrection'! And the Lycaonians thought Paul and Barnabas were themselves gods, and they wanted to worship them and offer sacrifices to them.

In our often inadequate efforts to communicate the gospel to people of different cultural or religious backgrounds, it is a comfort to see in Acts that the Holy Spirit gave considerable success to the apostles despite their communication failures. Fellowships of new Christian believers emerged both in Lystra (14:21) and Athens (17:34). As cross-cultural witnesses among ethnic minorities in our own country or as Christian workers overseas, we can easily become discouraged with a deep awareness that our fumbling efforts don't seem to scratch where people itch. How good to know that the Holy Spirit can work effectively through us despite our inadequacies!

The message

The apostolic message underlines the work of God for our salvation as well as the required human response. The underlying theme of Acts is always what Jesus by his Holy Spirit is doing in continuation of his work and teaching as recorded in Luke's Gospel (Acts 1:1, 2). Luke therefore underlines the powerful work of God in the message of the resurrection. And this goes hand in hand with the work of Jesus Christ in salvation and the forgiveness of sin.

In Acts 2:38, Luke gives his readers a brief synopsis of the apostolic message. In Christian witness today we need to take careful note of the model given to us in Acts. The vital elements are repentance, baptism, forgiveness of sins and receiving the gift of the Holy Spirit. The call to repentance features promi-nently in the Acts account of Christian witness. There can be no forgiveness of sins without a preceding repentance which renounces sin and turns from it. With the frequent call to repentance comes also the promise of 'forgiveness' (*aphesis*) with its basic sense of release from the dominion of sin. The word *aphesis* implies that sin holds an enslaving power over people, but Jesus offers release. While repentance and release from sin are the invisible working of the Holy Spirit in the heart of new believers, baptism represents the visible sign of entry into God's covenant and thus entry into the people of Christ. Baptism demonstrates publicly that the believer is now within God's covenant and belongs to Jesus Christ and his Church. This outward sign is further proved by God's gift of his Holy Spirit, which is commonly but not always accompanied by some spiritual gift like tongues.

Even at this very early stage, when the Church was confined to a Jewish and God-fearing membership, Peter already notes that the message of forgiveness and the gift of the Spirit are for *all* whom God calls, even for 'all who are far off' (2:39). The universality of the gospel and therefore of Christian mission is already evident.

In Acts 8:12, Luke summarises the message of Christian witness in different terms. Philip preached good news, which is defined as the kingdom of God and the name of Jesus Christ. Christians today may easily use the religious word 'gospel' without thinking of its real meaning. The gospel is not some rigid series of theological points without reference to the needs of non-Christians. We have always to ask what makes Jesus good news to particular people in their situations. For example, in a conference of East European Christian leaders I was asked to speak on 'What makes the gospel good news in a post-communist context? in an Eastern Orthodox context? in a Roman Catholic context? and in a post-modern context?' Returning from ten years in Asia to a village in England, we had to ask the same question.

In Acts 26:16–18, the resurrected Jesus tells Paul at his conversion that he must witness among both Jews and Gentiles. For both there is a precondition for receiving the forgiveness of sins and entry into the people of God who are sanctified by faith in Jesus. First they must turn from darkness to light, from the power of Satan to God. For those who use occult objects like magic books or tarot cards, these will need to be burned (19:19). Conversion is not only from sin to the Lord and his righteousness. It is also from the person of Satan to the person of the Lord. The rule of Satan leads inevitably to sin, while the lordship of Christ brings holiness and righteousness. Conversion means, therefore, a total break from Satan and sin in turning to the Lord and his righteousness. If we fail to teach about Satan in our evangelistic witness, new Christians may have trouble later in their Christian lives.

In the weeks between his resurrection and his ascension, Jesus taught his disciples about the kingdom of God (1:3). It is therefore not surprising that the kingdom of God lies at the heart of the apostles' preaching. This is closely linked to the early Church's baptismal confession 'Jesus is Lord'. God's kingdom is marked by the fact that Jesus reigns. And with Jesus as Lord, his standards of holiness must prevail in individual personal lives of moral holiness, in interpersonal relationships and within society. The reign of Jesus is also demonstrated by signs of God's power in action. When God's kingdom breaks into the world and Jesus is king, we may expect miracles.

In Acts, Luke refers frequently to 'the name' of Jesus Christ. Clearly he is influenced by the Old Testament use of 'the name of the Lord', referring to the overall person and character of God. Thus Israel sings praise to the name of the Lord (e.g. Psalm 7:17; 9:2). Israel trusted in his holy name (e.g. Psalm 33:21), knowing that the name of the Lord is great and holy. So in Acts the apostles preach the name of Jesus, and it is in his name that the power of God is released for healing (e.g. 3:6). Believers are baptised in the name of the Lord Jesus (e.g. 2:38; 19:5) and it is for this name that Christians willingly suffer shame (e.g. 5:41; 9:16). Indeed, it is uniquely by the name of Jesus Christ that people can be saved (4:12).

Acts 4:12 has been much quoted in the heated debate on pluralism and the Christian attitude to other faiths. Together with John 14:6, it has been used as the proof text for the traditional Christian view that salvation is only through faith in the death and resurrection of Jesus. Neither religious piety and zeal nor moral good works can be the means of salvation. The pluralist view that all religious faiths can bring their sincere followers to God for salvation undermines the very roots of evangelistic passion. Such a spirit of open-minded tolerance has led to the criticism that it is arrogant to think that Christians have the truth and should preach it to others. Particularly, evangelism among Jews and Muslims has become very controversial. It is fashionable to be tolerant of anything which seems tolerant, while at the same time being gravely intolerant of everything which appears to be in any way intolerant. The Jewish apostles in the New Testament, however, were firmly convinced of the absolute truth of the gospel of Jesus Christ. They did not hesitate to affirm that salvation is only by his name. And they proclaimed the good news of Jesus Christ both to their fellow Jews and more widely to the Gentiles.

In modern times, 'dialogue' has become the politically correct approach to mission. This word is, however, generally used without serious reference to its biblical background. As I have explained elsewhere (*What About Other Faiths?*, Hodder &

Stoughton, 1989), in his Gospel Luke only uses *dialogizomai* and *dialogismos*, which express a questioning uncertainty (e.g. 1:29; 5:21, 22), but in Acts he changes to *dialegomai*. In Acts, *dialegomai* ('dialogue') implies the use of discussional debate rather than monologue as the means of proclamation. The apostles, however, no longer reflect uncertainty concerning the message of Christ, but 'dialogue' (e.g. 17:2, 17; 19:9) with the definite aim of convincing and converting.

Acts 1:1 declares that the writings of Luke are 'the word': *logos*, which is translated in the NIV as 'book'. Throughout Acts 'the word' is emphasised. It is the word which the apostles preach, with the result that 'the word of God continued to increase and spread' (e.g. 12:24). In Paul's farewell to the Ephesian elders he commits them 'to God and to the word of his grace' (20:32). The modern denigration of words as untrustworthy contradicts the message of Acts. As we shall note again in John 1, God reveals himself and communicates to us by word. Likewise, Christian witnesses are called to communicate the glory of the Lord by means of words.

'Boldness' (parresia)

This word occurs frequently to describe the preaching and witness of the apostles. It has a two-fold meaning. Of course, it signifies a courageous openness of witness which flies in the face of all opposition and refuses to be silenced by the threat of persecution. Then, too, it implies a confident assurance of the truth of the message proclaimed. Courageously open witness requires a firm foundation of assurance of faith, for otherwise no one will dare to risk suffering and misunderstanding. Paul was very sure of his encounter with the risen Christ and therefore the reality of the resurrection. As a result, he was willing to suffer mob violence, beatings, prison and even death. Nothing could prevent him from witnessing boldly.

Of course, boldness must go together with wisdom – wise boldness or bold wisdom. Sadly, Europeans are often in danger of so stressing wisdom that boldness goes out of the window. Perhaps as Jews we are sometimes in danger of overplaying boldness to the neglect of wisdom. Both are needed together.

The apostles' boldness certainly did lead to fierce opposition. This was not only physical and violent, but was also evident in verbal criticism. Thus the Church was 'called a sect' (24:14). This word could sometimes be used less negatively (e.g. 26:5), but the usual usage was decidedly uncomplimentary (e.g. 28:22). In traditional Roman Catholic and Eastern Orthodox countries, Protestant churches are often derided as 'sects'. In Jewish societies too, messianic Jews are often called a 'sect'. In this way the enemies of the gospel attempt to make Christian witness sound so unworthy of serious consideration that people will not be drawn to the gospel of Jesus. Words can hurt us just as much as sticks and stones. Mockery and gentle sneers can shut the mouth of Christian witnesses just as effectively as the threat of prison or martyrdom. We need to pray for the Holy Spirit of Christ to inspire a renewed boldness among us.

The means

In a question-and-answer session among church leaders in Algeria a man asked me, 'Does not the history of the early Church in Acts give us a model for our church life and witness today?' A negative answer to such a question sounds unbelieving. But we have to ask how far Acts gives us a blueprint or model. Or is it merely giving us some principles which can then be applied to varying cultures and situations? Thus the early Church evidently based its worship on the model of the synagogue – must all Christian worship today follow that liturgical example exactly? People were healed by merely walking across the shadow of an apostle or touching a handkerchief – should we follow this form of healing ministry? In their witness the apostles majored on cultural centres and major cities – is tribal ministry therefore unbiblical? Unthinking literalism in applying Acts to modern mission may mislead us badly, but on the other hand we must ensure that our mission is based on the principles of God's word in Acts. Some of these include:

Teams

When Barnabas started on his mission outreach, he sought out Paul to be his companion. He did not go alone. At first it was Paul accompanying Barnabas, but later Paul took over the leadership. When they later clashed concerning whether John Mark should accompany them, two teams emerged with Paul and Barnabas as their respective leaders. At other times it was groups of Christians who went together and witnessed. One-man ministry was not the normal practice in Acts. This is surely a good principle for us. We all need fellow-workers to complement us, for none of us has all the needed gifts or a full-orbed personality.

Group decisions

Western culture tends to stress the individual above the group to which each belongs. So faith and conversion have to be individually experienced and all spiritual decisions are made on an individual basis. In Acts, however, not only are there cases of individual conversions, but also crowds of people came together into the Church of God (2:41; 4:4). Whole households made decisions together to turn to the Lord and be baptised (16:15, 33). As I have described in my life story, Life's Tapestry (O.M. Paternoster, 1997), our church in Indonesia experienced group movements to Christ in which a whole battalion of the army turned to Christ and were baptised, as did also a senior school and a hospital ward. Particularly in situations of intense persecution, it may prove almost impossible for one lone individual to become a Christian, but groups together can give greater security as well as mutual encouragement and fellowship. So, for example, in many Muslim societies, where Christian converts could well be murdered, we should be working and praying that whole families might come to faith together.

Mission support

In Corinth Paul stayed in the home of Aquila and Priscilla, who were tent-makers by profession. Although such work was despised because it dealt with the skins of dead animals, it seems that somehow Paul had also learned this skill (18:3) and so he worked with them while seeking to evangelise in the city. It would seem that Paul earned his living by his own hands when there was as yet no local church to support him. But we also know that when he had planted a living church in Macedonia they supported him financially (Phil. 4:10ff.). Is this a useful model for modern mission? Should cross-cultural mission workers support themselves when working in places where there is no local church? Should missionaries normally be supported by the receiving churches rather than by their home sending churches?

The present assumption that missionaries should be supported by their sending church stems from the colonial era, when mission was from the relatively wealthy Christian west to poorer countries overseas. But now the Church has become larger and stronger in many former 'mission fields' than in European countries. They may be poor financially, but they are rich in spiritual vitality, confidence of faith and with growing membership. But because they lack money they often remain recipients of western mission largesse. We rejoice in the tremendous growth of mission involvement from such dynamic churches as those of Latin America, Korea and Singapore. But if mission work overseas did not depend on financial wealth, the large but poorer churches of black Africa, India and the ex-communist countries could contribute even more significantly to worldwide mission.

Any change from the present system of home-church support would need to develop gradually, for otherwise the whole mission movement could be brought into chaos and badly disrupted. Such change needs to be introduced step by step.

Holistic mission

As we have seen, much mission talk today revolves around such jargon terms as 'the 10/40 window', 'adopt-a-people movement' and 'unreached peoples'. In his grace God has used such expressions to motivate people to more active involvement in evangelistic church-planting mission in some of the neediest parts of the world. But in Acts, mission is a much bigger calling than just church-planting evangelism. Paul also engaged in a long-term teaching ministry (e.g. 19:9–10; 20:31). He returned to churches he had planted in order to encourage and strengthen the Christians there. In Acts 20 he ministers to the elders of the church in Ephesus. In the 'Great Commission' in Matthew 28 we noted that mission involves not only basic evangelism among the unreached, but also laying down the external forms of the Church and teaching people to obey everything the Lord has commanded us. And in Luke's Gospel we saw that the task of mission includes not only preaching and teaching, but also social ministries for the poor and oppressed (Luke 4:18–19). So Luke has a broad picture of the task of witness and mission.

Conclusion

The final scene in Acts sees Paul in Rome, his ultimate destination and the heart of the empire. Here in his own home he was able to receive a wide variety of visitors and 'preached the kingdom of God and taught about the Lord Jesus Christ' (28:31). Paul's witness was bold and 'without hindrance'. With his bold testimony, nothing and no one could prevent the spread of the good news of Jesus Christ.

In declaring the gospel to Jewish leaders (28:17–28) he boldly stated that their rejection of the gospel was a fulfilment of Isaiah's prophecy (28:26–7). But, he affirmed, 'God's salvation has been sent to the Gentiles, and they will listen!' These final verses are open-ended and leave the reader with the impression that the story of Acts is only the beginning. Jesus will continue his work by his Holy Spirit throughout the history of the Church in the ever-widening expansion of the gospel. However, although mission revolved very largely around the Gentile nations, there has always been a remnant of faithful believing Jews – we should never forget that Paul and the other apostles were themselves Jewish.

Even in the early centuries of Christian history the witness of the gospel spread beyond the confines of 'the civilised world' around the shores of the Mediterranean. Following Paul's dream, it reached across to Spain and also along the North African coast. It followed the trade winds to India, moved north to the wild tribes of central and northern Europe, then east to the Caucasus and central Asia. The great wave of Nestorian mission even reached modern China, Indonesia and Japan as well as planting churches right across central Asia along the Silk Road. And so the history of Christian mission has moved on from generation to generation with ever-widening expansion of the Church. Failures, sin and setbacks have besmirched this great history of the ongoing work of the Lord Jesus by his Spirit, but nothing can stop the growth of the kingdom of God. 'Unhind-ered', Luke's final word in Acts (in the RSV translation), remains true. Now we in our day are called to fulfil our role as fellow-workers with Christ.

5

John's Gospel –
'By believing you
may have life'

In the past it was customary to encourage new believers to read John's Gospel on the assumption that people already had a fundamental knowledge of the life and teachings of Jesus as found in the first three Gospels. Now in western Europe, as in most parts of the world, such knowledge of the basics cannot be taken for granted. In our witness, therefore, it is usually wise to start with one of the first three Gospels rather than immediately recommending John. It was not John's purpose to teach the broad outline of Jesus' biography, for he knew that this had already been done by the previous Gospel writers. Yet it is increasingly recognised that John does record a historically accurate account of Jesus' life. He does not write chronologically, but takes care to emphasise what he wants his readers to understand. So he crafts his account around a series of miraculous signs linked to verbal teaching. Sign and word go together in conveying John's message.

Scholars debate when, where, how and by whom John's

Gospel was written. Our task in this book is rather to discern John's purpose and its significance for mission. John himself makes this clear in 20:31: 'that you may believe that Jesus is the Christ, the Son of God, and that by believing you may have life in his name'. So John declares that he has a double purpose in writing his Gospel. He wants his readers to gain an assured faith that Jesus is indeed the Messiah, God's Son. Then, too, he desires that people should find the reality of true life in and through Jesus Christ. As the good shepherd who opens the door to salvation and green pastures (10:9) he has come so that his followers may 'have life, and have it to the full'.

In 20:31 there is uncertainty concerning the tense of the verb 'believe'. Is it an aorist (used for an action that happened in the past and which is not repeated), signifying John's aim that people experience an initial life-changing conversion to Jesus? In that case the Gospel may be understood as an evangelistic tract. For example, the raising of Lazarus resulted in the disciples believing (11:15, aorist tense) and in Martha's confession of faith which parallels 20:31 (11:27, aorist tense). On the other hand, the verb 'believe' may be a continuous present tense, exhorting followers of Jesus to remain faithful and not backslide. Both views are seen to have support from within the Gospel itself.

Aorist – an evangelistic tract

D. Carson observes that John's readers had lived through the rise and fall of various false messiahs (cf. Acts 5:36–7). John is therefore demonstrating that Jesus really is the true Messiah, the Son of God. He is calling them to put their trust in Jesus. It is in relationship to Jesus that they can gain life. Right at the outset of his Gospel John stresses that life is found in Jesus (1:4), and this theme is repeated over and over again throughout the Gospel – as indeed also in John's first epistle. The well-known verse John 3:16 makes it clear that eternal life comes through believing in Jesus. Chapters 5 and 6 repeat the word 'life' many times to underline its central significance, for Jesus is the bread of life (6:48). Indeed, as we have seen, he has come with the set purpose that people might 'have life, and have it to the full' (10:10). This life comes through knowing the Father and Jesus himself (17:3). And this life is not merely for this world, but through faith in Jesus' death and resurrection believers are given eternal life (3:16, 36).

In persuading people to believe in Jesus as the Christ, John develops various contrasting pairs – e.g. life and death, life and judgment (3:36; 5:21–30), light and darkness, faith and unbelief, seeing and blindness, knowing and ignorance. These stark contrasts highlight the vital importance of coming to Jesus and the fearful danger of rejecting him. In all evangelistic mission it is necessary to demonstrate the darkness of unbelief as well as the glorious light of relating by faith with Jesus Christ.

Already in John 1:29–51 the reader is presented with an apologetic for the messiahship of Jesus. He is described as the Lamb of God (29–35), Son of God (34), Rabbi/Teacher (38), Messiah/Christ (41), King of Israel (49). So the evangelistic invitation is extended, 'Come and see' (39, 46; 4:29). Jesus is the end goal of those who seek (1:38; 18:4, 7; 20:15).

In his evangelistic appeal John also recounts testimonies of those who have come to faith in Jesus. At first Nicodemus comes to Jesus by night and fails to grasp what Jesus means by being born again. And Jesus seems to mock his initial words, 'We know you are a teacher who has come from God.' Jesus replies, 'We speak of what we know' (3:11) and chides Nicodemus as 'Israel's teacher' when he does not understand (3:10). But by 7:50 Nicodemus is daring to stand up against the fury of his fellow-Pharisees, yet still he does not make an open confession of faith. Finally, in 19:38–9 Nicodemus openly accompanies Joseph of Arimathea in burying Jesus and he brings a huge gift of myrrh and aloes. Conversion can be a gradual process, not always a dramatic Pauline Damascus Road experience.

Gradual conversion is seen also in the examples of the Samaritan woman and the blind man. The former engages in a lengthy discussion with Jesus before he reveals himself as the Messiah (4:26) and his mysterious knowledge of her marital situation finally convinces her. As her conversation with Jesus evolves, the realisation increasingly dawns on her that Jesus is the Messiah. In John 9, too, the blind man experiences Jesus' miracle-working power, comes to believe that he is a prophet (9:17) and that he is from God (9:33) and finally worships him as the Son of Man (9:38). John ends the account by implying that while the blind man could now see, the sighted Pharisees were actually blind. Their guilt therefore remains (9:41). So the reader is encouraged to see, know, understand, believe and worship. The reader may also note the warning not to reject Jesus. In John's Gospel the climactic rejection takes place when the people cry out for the crucifixion of Jesus, the Father's only-begotten Son, and the release of Bar-Abbas (literally 'son of the father'). Unbelief leads to fearful sin.

Present tense – no backsliding!

It is true that John underlines the necessity to come to Jesus, believe in him and receive his gift of life. That life is not only abundant (10:10), but also eternal (e.g. 3:16, 36). The conversion experience must lead to an ongoing relationship with Jesus and through him with the Father. A key word in John's Gospel is 'abide/remain'. As branches of the vine it is vital that believers remain in Jesus (15:1–11). As we remain in Christ, he promises to remain in us (15:4), and his words will also remain in us (15:7). Jesus keeps his Father's commandments and thus abides in his love. We are exhorted likewise to keep Jesus' commandments and abide in his love. The consequence is not just our own self-satisfaction with the comfort of resting in Jesus' love, but the emphasis remains on bearing fruit – indeed, 'much fruit'. And this fruit is also to endure and abide (15:16). So the works of the Father are done by the Son, and the works of the Son are done by his disciples. And the work of God progresses more and more. Christian mission consists of more than just evangelism with instantaneous conversions. Only ongoing abiding fruit fulfils God's purposes. When we preach or teach, we should pray that in five or ten years' time there will be definite fruit from today's work.

Keeping God's commandments and thus bearing fruit means loving one another (15:12, 17). While Christians live in the midst of a hostile world which hates them, they remain secure in the assurance of God's steadfast love and the cocoon of loving Christian relationships. It is in this context of the world's hatred that the disciples will receive the 'Counsellor . . . the Spirit of truth'. In Christ and by the Spirit we have the truth and are called to bear witness to it (15:26, 27). The word of Christ, the truth, the Spirit, loving one another, witness – Christian mission calls for these five to be kept firmly together in order to produce much fruit which will last.

Having fed the crowds with bread and fish, Jesus revealed himself as the living bread (6:35). Jesus' miracle inspired the crowds to desire to do God's work (6:28). Jesus explains to them that the work of God is to believe (continuous present tense) 'in the one he has sent'. However, Jesus also warns that one of the disciples will not persist in ongoing faith (6:64, continuous present tense). Jesus even challenges the disciples generally whether they too will be scandalised by his claim to be the bread of life. Will they also backslide and forsake him? Many had already drawn back and stopped following him (6:66–71).

John has more to say about Judas Iscariot than any of the other Gospel writers. In 12:1–8 Judas objects to Mary lavishing hugely expensive ointment on Jesus as she washes his feet. John comments that he was a thief, thus reminding his readers of the false shepherd who does not enter the sheepfold by the door, but climbs in some other way (10:1, 2). In 13:21–30 Jesus reassures Judas of his deep love by giving him the special morsel/ 'piece of bread', and at the same time shows his foreknowledge concerning Judas' plan to betray him. John comments that 'Satan entered into him' and dramatically closes the event with 'he went out. And it was night.' At the betrayal scene in chapter 18, Judas not only guides the soldiers and Jesus' enemies but is now also described as belonging to that company. He no longer finds his place among the followers of Jesus, but symbolically stands with Jesus' enemies (18:5). John has nothing further to say concerning Judas and does not mention him again. He is the ultimate example of a disciple who has backslidden and no longer believes. He is not even moved to repentance by Jesus' repeated application of the divine name 'YHWH'/'I am' to himself (18:5, 8).

The story of Peter's denial of Jesus stands in direct contrast to Judas' betrayal. Although stricken with fear and thus falling into a seemingly bottomless pit of failure, Peter still believes in Jesus and still loves him. Even before his final restoration by the risen Jesus (21:15ff.), Peter still remains with the other disciples (20:2) and he is the first to enter the empty tomb. At the conclusion of Peter's restoration, after he has been instructed to care for and feed the Lord's sheep, Jesus commands him: 'Follow me!' (continuous present tense). Peter had already begun to follow Jesus, had failed him and been restored. Now he is to continue the ongoing process of believing and following – even if the climax of his discipleship would be following Jesus and glorifying God in crucifixion (21:19).

After the first sign of turning water into wine many 'believed in his name' (2:23), but Jesus did not trust them because he knew their fallible natures and their tendency to backslide. While the fickle crowds in John 6 and then Judas himself are clear examples of this danger, Christians are encouraged by the knowledge that Jesus himself is our shepherd. He knows and cares for his sheep. They belong to him and he lays down his life so that they may gain true life. His sheep hear his voice and follow him (10:3, 4, 16, 27; cf. 3:29).

My wife and I have happy memories of visiting her brother-in-law's sheep farm in New Zealand. Although he possessed 1,400 sheep, he seemed to know them all personally and they responded trustingly to his voice. To us as city-dwellers the sheep all looked alike and lacked personal individual characters, but to him each one was loved and special. We were challenged in our missionary calling to be under-shepherds in caring for the Lord's flock.

As C. Wright points out in his *The Message of Ezekiel* (IVP, 2001), John 10 is not merely teaching that Jesus 'could be nice to poor lost lambs'! Jesus is clearly relating not only to Psalm 23, but also to Ezekiel 34 which boldly asserts that the lost sheep have no true king. This was a bold, even treasonable, charge when Israel in Jesus' time was ruled by King Herod. No wonder some felt that Jesus was either mad or demon-possessed (10:19–21)! Ezekiel also castigates the false shepherds who feed themselves instead of caring for their sheep. The Pharisees and other leaders of Israel will hardly have enjoyed Jesus' reference to Ezekiel! And in Ezekiel 34:15 the Lord declares that he himself will be the shepherd for his sheep. Now Jesus states that he is the good shepherd, thus claiming to be YHWH himself. And YHWH outlines in considerable detail how he will tend and lovingly care for his scattered flock.

It should also be noted that in Ezekiel 34:13 YHWH says that he will gather his flock 'out from the nations', thus widening the horizons beyond the borders of Israel. This reminds God's people always to lift up their eyes and see beyond the limited horizons of their own land and people.

With his gift of eternal life comes the promise that his sheep 'shall never perish' (10:28). They belong to the Father who is greater than all, so no one can succeed in snatching them out of his hand. Jesus will 'lose none' of all the Father has given him (6:39). What assurance this gives to insecure Christian believers! Thanks to the Lord's abiding care we can continue in faith even to the end.

'Jesus is the Christ, the Son of God' (20:31)

As we have already noted, John's purpose in writing his Gospel is so that people may believe that Jesus is the Christ, the Son of God. So he introduces us to people who early on took this step of faith. Even before Jesus raises Lazarus from the grave, Martha responds with faith to the claims of Jesus to be the resurrection and the life (11:25–7). While the dead body of Lazarus still languishes in the tomb, she boldly declares that she believes in Jesus as 'the Christ, the Son of God' – exactly the same words as in 20:31. Clearly John connects closely the death and raising of Lazarus with the death and resurrection of Jesus himself. Martha's faith foreshadows the new assurance of faith among the disciples at the resurrection of Jesus. And this in turn encourages John's readers and people throughout succeeding history to believe that Jesus is indeed the true Messiah and Saviour of the world.

Martha's profession of faith is followed immediately by her going to her sister with the good news of Jesus. Likewise, as we shall see, 20:31 leads straight into the story of Jesus enabling his disciples to catch a 'large number of fish'. This symbolic story of fishing plus the call to Peter to follow Jesus in shepherding and feeding his flock conclude John's Gospel. Thus a declaration of faith in Jesus as the Christ is not an end in itself. It must lead to the two-fold task of mission in fishing and shepherding.

We note that, unlike the other Gospels, John shows particular interest in Philip. As a follower of Jesus he is a model for the Church. Although he does not always understand what Jesus means (6:7; 14:8, 9), he knows that Jesus is the long-awaited Messiah foretold by Moses and the prophets. With this faith he brings other people to Jesus (1:45, 46; 12:21, 22).

In order that his readers may come to definite ongoing faith in Jesus, John makes a point of demonstrating the reliability of the claim that Jesus is the Christ sent by the Father. Thus in 5:33–7 Jesus stresses the reliability of the witness to himself because he does not testify about himself. It is the Father himself and the Scriptures which testify to him. And their witness is supported by John the Baptist and the work which the Father gave him to do. Likewise in 10:24ff., Jesus' miracles 'speak for him' and those who are his sheep hear his voice. Jesus' oneness with the Father finally demonstrates that he is indeed the Messiah, the one who has been sent by the Father. In 8:12ff., Jesus declares that his testimony is valid because he knows where he comes from and where he is going. And his Father joins forces with him in his testimony and glorifies him.

Going beyond the amazing fact that Jesus is the promised Messiah, chapter 8 concludes with the staggering claim 'before Abraham was born, I am'. Using the divine name YHWH/'I am', Jesus declares that he is not only one with the Father, but also co-eternal in his divine nature. No wonder the Jewish leaders who rejected him wanted to stone him! But this claim of Jesus lies at the very heart of the Christian message.

In his Gospel, John is showing that as Messiah and Son of God Jesus transcends everything good in the Old Testament. He is greater than Abraham or Moses. The temple finds its fulfilment in his body and so the Feast of Dedication points to him. Likewise, the sacrifices climax in him as the Lamb of God. In the same way, the Passover points to him, as do also the other Jewish holy days. He is the living bread of the Passover and his death significantly took place at Passover. He is the light of the world and from him streams of living water flow – the symbols of the Feast of Tabernacles. Some commentators have even suggested that John structures his Gospel around the Jewish holy days, seeing Jesus transcending them all.

But the greatest way in which John shows Jesus fulfilling the Old Testament is in the 'I am' sayings. Ultimately Jesus is not only the holy days, temple, sacrifice, Law and other things in perfection, he is also YHWH himself come into the world. He is personally the great shepherd of the sheep. He is the Lord God incarnate. It is in him that his disciples are called to put their faith. It is he to whom they are to witness.

The Prologue (1:1–18)

'John's Gospel in a nutshell': the Prologue is often described in this way. Many of the main themes begin their journey through the Gospel in these early verses.

The first verse begins with the words 'In the beginning', reminding us of the first creation in Genesis 1. In this way John declares that Jesus brings the new creation and ushers in the new era of the kingdom of God. In the Old Testament the fact of creation was commonly used (e.g. 2 Kgs. 19:15; Ps. 24:1, 2) to demonstrate that God is Lord over all nations, not just Israel. Creation is the beginning of all nations' history, not just the history of Israel. So the creator God desires to be Lord over all. The call to worldwide mission therefore has its foundations in the fact of creation. And in these early verses creation is linked to the repeated emphasis on 'all' and 'the world'.

All things were created by the word. And the life of the word is the light of all humans. Indeed, the light shines not only in Israel, but particularly in the darkness of the world which is outside God's covenant and which is fundamentally in opposition to him. So the true light enlightens *everybody*, for God's purpose is that 'through him all people might believe' (1:7).

John proceeds to underline the word 'world' by repeating it four times – Jesus 'was coming into the *world*', 'he was in the *world*', 'the *world* was made through him', 'the *world* did not recognise him' (1:9, 10). In these two verses John again reminds his readers of the first creation. In the Genesis account, however, the word 'world' is not used. God created the heavens and the *erets*/'earth'. Already by New Testament times, and still today, the word *erets*/'earth' related to *erets Israel*/'the land of Israel'. John is specifically wanting to widen his readers' horizons from their nationalistic blinkers. He therefore stresses *the world*, not just *erets*/earth – and does so by four-fold repetition. God's purposes reach out to bring life and light to all nations, not just to Israel.

Sadly, however, 'the world did not recognise him' and even his own people 'did not receive him'. The pathos of this last statement that Jesus' own people rejected him reminds us of the urgent call still today to work and pray for the evangelisation of the Jewish people. Although God wants his light to shine out to all peoples everywhere, the Gospel shows how he is universally rejected by both Jews and Gentile Romans. Nevertheless the promise remains that all (whether Jew or Gentile) can become God's children if they receive his Son Jesus Christ and believe in him (1:12). In Old Testament times only Jews and proselytes could be children of God, but now the door is opened to all. Adoption as God's children no longer depends on 'natural descent' in being children of Abraham, Isaac and Jacob. It is now God alone who brings us to birth as his children (1:13).

In a reminder of the Old Testament concept of wisdom (Prov. 8:1–23) John proceeds from creation to 'the Word'. Debate has raged concerning the nature of the word, whether it is fully human, fully divine or partly both. Important though these debates were in the first centuries of the Christian Church, they would not seem to have been in John's mind – and they hardly relate to modern apologetic debates! John was more interested in an Old Testament and Jewish view of 'the Word' than such Greek debates. In Jewish thought, words create and reveal. God spoke a word and creation came into being. And it is by his spoken and written words that he reveals himself. As Christians too we need to be God-like in our use of words, making sure that they are aimed at accomplishing something and that they reveal rather than conceal our thoughts.

The Word, John says, was *pros* – 'with' – God. Although this preposition is used to mean 'with', it also carries the sense of 'towards'. Relationship with someone always implies a moving towards that person. In our union with Jesus Christ we too are incorporated with him into close unity with the Father. Likewise, the task of mission is to draw people increasingly towards Jesus and thus into an intimate relationship *with* him and the Father.

The other three Gospels recount how Jesus was born in a particular Jewish family and they give considerable specific details. In John's Gospel, however, no specific cultural context is given, but 'the Word became flesh'. Again, John is emphasising that Jesus came not just for Israel, but more widely for all the world.

While Greek thought overemphasised the spirit to the neglect of the flesh, John, and indeed the whole New Testament, dignifies the body and material things. Jesus was not just some incorporeal spirit, but fully human. The temple with the very presence of God is found in his physical body. Material and physical things have importance in the Christian faith. Our bodies are the temple of the living God and are to be respected, honoured and cared for. Mission must relate also to material needs, not just to the soul.

Verses 14 to 18 of chapter 1 echo the exodus story and reveal Jesus as the greater Moses. He tabernacles among us, full of grace and truth (Exod. 34:6) which outshines the Law of Moses. He comes from the Father (a common theme in John's Gospel), shines with the glory of God and uniquely reveals the Father. It is therefore only through Jesus that we can know God, receiving grace and truth. As Christian witnesses, too, we are to walk in his footsteps. We should be characterised by grace and truth, reflect the glory of the Lord in our lives and reveal the Father through the Son by the Holy Spirit.

Cleansing the temple (2:12–22)

All four Gospel writers tell the story of Jesus clearing the temple of the money-changers and people selling animals for the sacrifices. But unlike the other Gospels, John places this event right at the outset of Jesus' ministry, immediately after the very first sign in which Jesus turned water into wine (2:1–11). So John sets the tone for his whole Gospel. Just as Jesus converts plain water into the very best wine, so also he cleanses the temple and changes it from being a mere 'market' (2:16) into being the house of prayer God intended it to be.

The clearing of the temple also implied that the temple's days were numbered. It could be temporarily returned to its proper function of being a place of prayer, but with the coming of Immanuel/'God with us', the perfect atoning sacrifice, it already faced destruction as a redundant relic of the pre-messianic age. Like the other Gospel writers, John devotes considerable space in his Gospel to the death of Jesus as the climax and purpose of his life. As the final and perfect Lamb of God he makes all other blood sacrifices unnecessary. Israel would no longer be tempted to presume security and salvation on the basis of having the temple in her midst. Neither the presence of God nor the shedding of blood in sacrifice for sin would be located any longer in a building made by human hands.

Having cleansed the temple and facing the wrath of the Jewish leaders, Jesus prophesied that he would raise the temple again in three days. In this way he pointed forwards to his own death and resurrection. His body was the new temple: on the cross it would be destroyed, but after three days it would be raised again by the Father in the resurrection.

Referring to Isaiah 56:7, Mark notes that the noisy bustle of the temple's business transactions took place in the Court of the Gentiles, the one part of the temple which was open for the Gentiles to worship God in. Perhaps John, as also Matthew and Luke, assume this fact. Certainly it remains true that in ridding the temple of its market atmosphere Jesus makes it possible for the Gentiles also to worship and pray to the God of Israel. It is therefore a sign that his ministry is for all nations. As he turns ordinary water into wine, so he makes the Gentiles who are 'no people' the very people of God. The Gentiles too can now be 'born of God' (1:13).

All peoples

It is commonly asserted that in John's Gospel there is a succession of miraculous signs followed by sections of verbal explanation. For example, in chapter 5 Jesus heals a man and then comes teaching that true life comes through Jesus. In chapter 6 Jesus feeds the Jewish crowd and then explains that he is the bread of life. The raising of Lazarus is followed by the word that Jesus is the life and the resurrection. So, as we saw in Acts, sign and word go hand in hand together. Mission does not merely consist of verbal preaching and teaching, but also a healing ministry with visible signs of God's grace and love.

While in John 1–12 the sign always precedes the explanatory word, in the final climax of the Gospel this changes. To mark the pre-eminent importance of the final death and resurrection of Jesus, John presents his readers with a word sandwich. The long section of teaching in chapters 14–17 is bracketed within two connected signs – the washing of feet and the actual cross and resurrection. As we align our lives to God's mission statement, humble service and obedient sacrifice for the salvation of the world become vitally significant.

How does John introduce this climactic event of Jesus' crucifixion and resurrection? The introductory chapters leading up to the crucifixion conclude with the coming of the Greeks to see Jesus (12:20ff.). As Gentiles, they were evidently somewhat uncertain whether Jesus would be willing to receive them. They therefore went first to Philip, drawn perhaps by his Greek-sounding name and by the fact that he came from the rather Gentile Bethsaida of Galilee. Was Philip also uncertain whether Jesus would receive them? Certainly he went first to Andrew, and then they went together to Jesus (like small children going hesitantly to their headmaster?).

Jesus' reaction to the coming of the Greeks seems at first sight to be right over the top – 'The hour has come for the Son of Man to be glorified.' Jesus then proceeds to talk excitedly about a grain of wheat bearing much fruit when it dies. When he is lifted up from the earth, he will draw all people to himself (12:32). The word 'all' reminds us of the Prologue. Jesus has not only come for his own Jewish people, but through his death and resurrection he will draw people from every nation and race to himself.

The coming of the Gentile Greeks to Jesus fulfils the Old Testament hope that the Gentiles would be drawn in to Zion to worship the God of Israel. Under the old covenant, Israel was not sent out to the Gentiles to preach to them, but should so live out the glory and holiness of God that the Gentiles would be attracted in. Now Jesus transcends and is the climactic perfection of Zion and the temple with its sacrifices and the presence of God. So when Gentiles come to Jesus, they are fulfilling the prophecy of Gentiles coming to Zion and thus to God himself.

When Jesus sees this fulfilment of the Old Testament expectation, he excitedly recognises that the time has come for the final denouement. He can now move on to the cross and resurrection, through which people of all nations will come to the Father and find life.

The supreme significance of the cross is underlined by Jesus' constant reference through John's Gospel to 'my hour'. The cross is also seen as Jesus' final glory. So he responds to the coming of the Greeks by describing his death as the hour for the Son of Man to be glorified. As may be observed again and again throughout the New Testament, the Christian faith is centred on a great paradox. Jesus' utter shame and humiliation with the ignominy of his trial and crucifixion is actually his ultimate glory. It is the crucial end-time 'hour', the commencement of the new era of the kingdom of God. And Jesus' kingdom is for all nations and peoples. The Church's task in the new era is to witness to the crucified and risen Jesus and bring his kingdom to all the world.

John unhesitatingly presents us with Jesus' uniqueness as the only God-sent means of salvation. In 3:3 Jesus states that no one can see the kingdom of God unless they are born again. Such new life is found through faith in the risen Christ. Without faith in Jesus no one can experience for themselves the glory of the kingdom. It will remain an abstract theological or social theory. Even more boldly, Jesus affirms that he is 'the way and the truth and the life' and even adds the exclusive claim that 'no-one comes to the Father except through me' (14:6). Some liberal writers (e.g. P. Knitter and J. Hick) have suggested that these words are mere exaggerated words of love – the way a child may say of its mother that 'my Mum is the best mother in the world'. But Jesus is saying these words about himself, not about someone else. Their stark simplicity does not allow for any compromise. Jesus is clearly claiming total uniqueness as the one and only way to his Father. Only in him can absolute truth be found. And in him alone can people discover the reality of life abundant. In the modern climate of pluralism such exclusive claims sound terribly politically incorrect and intolerant. We have to ensure that the exclusive claims of Jesus and our assurance of absolute truth in Jesus Christ go hand in hand with a humble, learning attitude towards people of other faiths. Humble, learning dialogue can go together with loving certainty of faith and therefore a clear and definite witness (see M. Goldsmith, *What About Other Faiths?*, Hodder & Stoughton, 1989).

The Samaritans

Although the best of rabbinic teaching always foresaw that the kingdom of heaven would be universal for all peoples, it was often asserted that the kingdom is really just for three sorts of people. Leading rabbis taught that under the branches of the kingdom tree the birds of the air would find shade. These birds represented all nations and peoples. But commonly in Jewish thought it was considered that the kingdom was only for men (not women), only for the righteous (not sinners) and only for Jews (not others). John 4 comes therefore as a radical reversal of such prejudiced thinking.

Throughout the chapter John repeats the word 'the woman' to underline the significance of the fact that Jesus revealed himself so clearly to a woman. Even his disciples were surprised to find him talking with a woman (4:27). Likewise the account brings out clearly that this woman was publicly known for her immorality in having had a variety of men in her life. Indeed, Jesus bluntly told her that her present partner was not her husband. However, Jesus' kingdom is for women as well as men, for sinners and not just for the righteous. It is also for Samaritans, as we have noted earlier. Being half-Jewish and half-Gentile, the Samaritans form a bridge between the Jews and the Gentiles. So this chapter opens the door for wider mission, crossing all barriers and reaching out to people of every background. As followers of Jesus, Christians are called to share his vision for his kingdom.

Jesus' conversation with the Samaritan woman demonstrates real understanding and patience as he gradually leads her towards his great confession: 'I am he' – once again taking to himself the divine title 'I am'/YHWH. After she heard this declaration, she left her water jar in order to go into the city to tell others about Jesus. Commentators see this as a model for Christian disciples. We too should leave everything in order to go and witness for Jesus. Her faith was still somewhat uncertain, asking the question: 'Could this be the Christ?' Nevertheless 'many of the Samaritans' came to believe in Jesus because of her testimony (4:39). In the grace of God, even weak faith can yield an abundant harvest. As the story develops, however, many more came to faith in Jesus because they heard his own teaching and testimony (4:41, 42) – and their faith was clear: 'we know that this man really is the Saviour of the world'.

So the Samaritan woman gives us the model for mission. Her faith led immediately to her abandoning everything in order to tell others about Jesus. At first people come to faith in Jesus because of her testimony, but after a while Jesus 'stays' with them and they meet with him for themselves. So they base their faith directly on his words. The Christian witness is merely a middle-man to introduce people into a personal relationship with the Lord himself. John the Baptist also exemplified this principle.

In the middle of this chapter John interposes some key teaching about mission (4:31–8). While the disciples were only thinking of material food, Jesus declared with deeper meaning that he had other, more important food. 'My food . . . is to do the will of him who sent me and to finish his work.' Jesus' heartfelt desire and life purpose was to do the Father's work. He did not come to earth to fulfil his own dreams or follow his own interests. He was entirely dedicated to doing the will of God. As his followers we should have the same aim in life.

It is noteworthy that Jesus not only started the work of God but also determined to 'finish' it. In this he showed his oneness with the Father, for God not only begins a good work in us, but also brings it to completion (Phil. 1:6). It is the character of God not only to start a work, but also to continue it and bring it to its fulfilment. In mission, too, Christians are not only concerned to start work with initial church planting and evangelism, but their mission goes on to bring churches to maturity with good biblical teaching and training. The aim is to present every Christian to the Lord 'without stain or wrinkle or any other blemish, but holy and blameless' (Eph. 5:27).

In verse 35 of chapter 4 Jesus proceeds to contrast his thinking with that of his disciples. 'Do *you* not say . . . ?' reveals their less urgent concern for mission. 'Four months more and then the harvest' – in their opinion there is no desperate hurry for the harvest. But Jesus declares that the fields are *now/already* ripe for harvest. Living in a village, I have observed that farmers work day and night when the harvest is ripe – they do not take a holiday in Majorca at that time! The task is urgent! Jesus shows that he is speaking about mission, for the harvest for which the sower and reaper work is 'for eternal life'. In the other Gospels Jesus states that the angels in heaven rejoice when a lost sheep is found. Now he declares that human sowers and reapers rejoice together when the harvest is gathered in. And the worldwide mission task has already begun with the ministry of Jesus and of his disciples.

In Christian mission some labour in the heavy task of primary evangelism, sowing the seed and often seeing very little fruit. Others come later and reap the harvest which was prepared by those who sowed with sweat and tears. It is noticeable that Christians often honour the reapers above the sowers. I have observed that if I talk about my rugged and apparently unfruitful work as a pioneer Muslim evangelist in south Thailand, people easily dismiss me as boringly old-fashioned with no knowledge of the fullness of God's Spirit! On the other hand, if I talk about the mass movement in Indonesia with thousands coming to faith in Christ and experiencing radical change in their lives, I am welcomed as someone who really knows the power of the Spirit. Actually I was just as bad and unspiritual a missionary in Indonesia as I had been in south Thailand! I did not experience a revival on the plane between the two!

The word 'together' (4:36) is also significant. Christian witnesses with very different ministries need to learn to work and rejoice together in unity. In his prayer (17:11, 21, 23) Jesus stresses the need for unity among Christians. Through this unity the world will come to know that Jesus is indeed the Messiah sent by the Father. Disunity hinders the witness of the gospel. It therefore comes as something of a shock to discover the empire-building self-glorification of some churches, denominations and mission workers in their mission overseas. They seem sometimes to be spreading their own name rather than that of the Lord, to be underlining their particular theological or worship peculiarities rather than the necessity of faith in Jesus and commitment to him. The missions which work for partnership deserve our support.

Always at work

After Jesus had healed a man by the pool of Bethsaida he uttered the enigmatic words, 'My Father is always at his work . . . and I, too, am working' (5:17). Jesus had purposely done his miracle on the Sabbath, although he could easily have waited an extra day before healing the man. After all, he had been ill for thirty-eight years, so one day more or less would not have been too serious! Jesus could have waited until the Sunday instead of provoking controversy by doing this miraculous work on the Sabbath, but he specifically courted the Jewish authorities' opposition. The ensuing debate allowed him to give his teaching.

The Jewish leaders at that time seem to have debated whether God himself worked on the Sabbath. Some declared that God is so perfectly holy that he cannot possibly break his Law, so he must rest on the Sabbath without doing any work. Others, however, observed that the very existence of the world depends on the constant providence of God, so it is impossible for God to twiddle his thumbs even for a second. Jesus enters right into the midst of this argument. He declares that his Father is always working, he never stops. And he then proceeds to place himself together with his Father in asserting that he too, like his Father, is constantly working.

In Christian mission there are times and places when it is

hard to discern the working of God. When there is little or no response of faith from those with whom one is working, it is easy to lose one's assurance that God really is working out his purposes. When Christian workers hear dynamic reports of God mightily at work by his Spirit in some other part of the world, it is not easy to persevere in ministry which seems to be hitting its head against a brick wall. It can then be encouraging to rest one's weary soul on the pillow of Jesus' assurance that he, like his Father, is constantly at work.

It is noteworthy how John describes the healed man immediately telling other people about what Jesus had done for him. We have already observed this emphasis in John's Gospel. The experience of Jesus' healing salvation leads directly into witness. This principle should govern all Christian discipleship.

John has sometimes been accused of anti-semitism because of his use of the expression 'the Jews' when talking of Jesus' enemies. However, John himself was Jewish, as were also all the first Christians and their apostolic leaders. And John knew that Jesus himself was a Jew. It is unthinkable that John could possibly have been anti-semitic. His use of 'the Jews' is typical of the manner in which some minority groups speak of their own people when they are bitterly opposed by the majority. 'The Jews' relates particularly to the Jewish leaders of that time, but perhaps also to the crowds who followed the leaders in opposing the first Christians.

Indeed, it is interesting that the Sabbath healing, with its ensuing controversy with 'the Jews', is followed by Jesus' teaching that he gives life to those who believe in him (5:16–47). This leads immediately into the feeding of the Jewish crowd of five thousand men plus women and children (6:1ff.). If John had been anti-semitic, as some critics assert, he would surely not have recorded the feeding of the Jewish crowd. He would have concentrated on the Gentile crowd of four thousand. In Matthew's Gospel the feeding of the Jewish crowd was preceded by the martyrdom of John the Baptist, underlining to Jesus his own imminent sacrificial death. John's Gospel places the miraculous feeding of the Jewish crowd in the context of the 'Jewish Passover Feast' (6:4), and this also relates the feeding of the crowd to Jesus' atoning death as the Lamb of God, the ultimate sacrifice for the sins of the world. Again, it should be noted that Jesus' model is not only to feed people with physical food, but also with the spiritual reality of his sacrificial death. In the context of John 5:16ff. Jesus has come to bring eternal life to all who hear his word and 'believe him who sent me' (5:24). He is the bread of life.

Who is blind and who sees? (9:1–41)

With its repeated emphasis on 'see' and 'believe', this passage has obvious mission significance. The increasing faith of the blind man contrasts with the unbelieving blindness of the Pharisees. So the blind man's 'Lord, I believe' shines brightly against the Pharisees' 'Are we blind too?' Jesus points out that blindness carries no condemnation, but guilt falls on those who claim to see but do not believe (9:41).

We have already observed how the blind man witnesses to what has happened to him through the miraculous work of Jesus. Although Jesus had clearly declared, 'I am the light of the world', the blind man does not at first understand who Jesus is. Nevertheless, he testifies to the fact that Jesus healed him and asserts that 'he is a prophet'. And Jesus' confession that he is the Son of Man elicits an immediate response of faith.

Witness incurs fierce opposition. Three times in John the threat of being put out of the synagogue (*aposunagogos*) hangs over those who stand for Jesus (9:22; 12:42; 16:2). By the time John's Gospel was written, this threat had surely become a sad reality for Jewish witnesses to Jesus as the Messiah/Christ. And throughout Christian history it has remained true for all faithful witnesses to Jesus that persecution and opposition hang over us like a sword of Damocles. Such persecution may take various forms – for the Jewish Christian, as also for many others who convert from another religion, it may well involve exclusion from their community. It can sometimes mean being thrown out of the family, too. In many Muslim societies, conversion to Jesus Christ may well lead to martyrdom. In nominally Christian societies, witness may only result in curled-lip mockery or discrimination in job promotion. But caustic words and economic discrimination can hurt almost as badly as sticks and stones, prison camps and martyrdom.

John notes that the blind man's parents were happy to testify that he was their son, that he was born blind and that he could now see. But 'we don't know' how the miracle took place or who healed him. This careful ignorance was because 'they were afraid of the Jews' (9:22) – again, the term 'the Jews' does not imply anti-semitism, for the blind man and his parents were also Jewish. John shows how the parents avoided danger for themselves but did not hesitate to put their son into a position of confrontation with the Pharisees (9:23). Christian witness and the possibility of suffering for Christ separate true believers from others, even within one's own family.

The chapter begins with the pressing question of whose fault it was that the man had been born blind – his own or his parents' sin? Believers in the doctrine of reincarnation would unhesitatingly declare that his blindness was due to his own sin, either in his present life or in a previous incarnation. Thus the former English football coach was sacked because of his stated belief that the physically handicapped suffered as a result of their own evil deeds. The 'tolerant' English public could not tolerate the traditional Buddhist and Hindu belief in reincarnation when it was clearly spelled out in that way!

But Jesus unequivocally declares that the man's blindness was not the result of sin at all. In the providence of God even this suffering was 'so that the work of God might be displayed in his life' (9:3). What a challenge to us all when we face the dilemma of suffering! We should not blame God with the unbelieving question, 'How can a loving God allow it?' Our response to tragedy and pain is to look for God to manifest his work in us.

How are we sent? (20:21)

'As the Father has sent me, I am sending you.' John notes the direct line in the continuum of sending. The Father sent the Son – the Son sends his disciples and then his people throughout the history of the Church. Of course, the Son also joins the Father in sending the Holy Spirit. Each in turn lives and works in order to do the will of the one who sends them. Thus Jesus desires to fulfil the will and work of the Father. The Holy Spirit's function is likewise to glorify the Son and continue his work. As followers of Jesus, we too are sent in order to take on his saving work for the sake of all peoples.

Jesus declares that he is sending his disciples out in the same way the Father sent him. Inevitably we are bound to ask how the Father sent his Son and so gain accurate insight into the task of mission into which the Son sends us. But first we need to look at the context of these words.

The disciples' situation was desperate. They had given up everything in order to follow Jesus as their rabbi and Messiah. But now he had been ignominiously tried and crucified. Could they continue to believe in him? Over the previous decades there had been various false messiahs whom the crowds had followed. Then these false messiahs had been killed by the Romans and their movements had evaporated like morning mist.

What shame it would bring to have to crawl back to their families and friends with the admission that they had made a terrible mistake! So now they huddled together on the first Sunday of Christian history with 'the doors locked for fear of the Jews' (20:19, 26). If the Jewish authorities and the Romans had killed Jesus, it was very possible that they would search out his followers and crucify them too. No wonder they were afraid as well as bewildered and disillusioned. As they gathered together on that Sunday, did they praise the Lord with loud cries of hallelujah and with songs of praise? I doubt it! It is more likely that an embarrassed silence reigned as they stood around aimlessly.

It is into this situation that we get the amazing words, 'Jesus came and stood among them' (20:19, 26). Whenever I preach on this passage, a tingle of excitement goes down my spine! I picture the resurrected Jesus suddenly standing next to me as I preach and asking whether he might be allowed to listen in. Equally, I think of him standing physically in front of the congregation, thanking them for worshipping him and praying to him, but asking if he might please listen to our singing and praying. Would his physical presence change our preaching or our worship and prayer? Of course, we know by faith that Jesus does indeed stand among us spiritually by his Holy Spirit, but somehow the physical presence of the risen Lord feels different.

Before the Lord can call his followers to effective outgoing mission, we need to have met with him in such a life-changing way that fear and discouragement melt into deep joy – 'the disciples were overjoyed when they saw the Lord' (20:20).

Three times John records that Jesus greeted his disciples with the traditional *shalom*/'peace be with you' (20:19, 21, 26). John is thus noting the significance of the everyday greeting, *shalom*. In their situation of danger, with the temptation to disillusionment, they needed that inner peace which God alone can give by his Spirit. In their future mission they would face further times of extreme danger. Discouragement and the temptation to disillusionment can also be a common experience among Christians involved in mission. God's gift of peaceful inner harmony (*shalom*) is a vital prerequisite for the life of mission.

The essential requirement for the call to mission, however, lies in receiving the Holy Spirit. As Jesus sends his disciples out to carry on his work, he breathes on them and says, 'Receive the Holy Spirit.' We may parallel this with Acts 1:8, where receiving the Holy Spirit and being Christ's witnesses among all peoples are inseparably connected.

We may note that in John 20 Jesus' sending of his disciples precedes the giving of the Holy Spirit. In Acts 1 the reverse is true: receiving the power of the Holy Spirit is the necessary precondition for the call to international mission. Both are true.

We need the Holy Spirit before we dare to move out into the task of worldwide mission. Likewise, we have to confess that without the indwelling power of Jesus by his Holy Spirit we can do nothing and our mission work will always remain frustrating and ineffective. As we get involved in this great adventure and move out into mission, we desperately need to call on the Lord to fill and empower us with his Holy Spirit.

By his Holy Spirit Jesus goes with us in being sent out in his work. Just as he was sent into the world to save his people from their sins (Matt. 1:21), so by his indwelling Spirit we are sent out with the authoritative message of the forgiveness of sins. And the dark side of that ministry also leads to the condemnation of those who reject the message of Jesus and do not receive his forgiveness – 'they are not forgiven' (20:23).

Having noted something of the context of 20:21 and the fundamental task into which Jesus sends us, we turn now to the actual words: 'As the Father has sent me, I am sending you.' This verse contains the final usage of the term 'send' which is so much a feature of John's Gospel. It is used not only of Jesus being sent by the Father, but also frequently of John the Baptist and of the disciples. The verb 'send' relates to the noun 'apostle', one who is sent by God with a mission. And as the Roman Catholic commentator R.E. Brown points out in his Anchor Bible commentary (Geoffrey Chapman, 1966), this verse cannot be used to confine the title 'apostle' only to the eleven disciples, for this title was used much more widely in the early Church. All followers of Jesus should be available to hear Jesus' call to be sent out into the world in mission. Although John changes the word used for 'send' when referring to the commissioning of the disciples, the verbs 'stand in parallelism here with no visible sign of distinction' (R.E. Brown). The disciples are sent out in the same way as the Father sent Jesus.

How then was Jesus sent? This question demands a whole series of books and we cannot possibly answer it adequately here. But we may note that while he was sent to his own Jewish people, his ministry also touched the Samaritans and the Gentiles.

His vision extended to all peoples. Although he was called only to the lost sheep of the house of Israel (Matt. 15:24), we have seen that the context of that verse reveals the international nature of Jesus' calling. That must be true also of Christians today.

The basic purpose of Jesus' coming into the world was to bring salvation from sin to his people. He was also deeply aware of others' needs and worked to provide for them. So he fed the crowds, healed the sick, cast out demons and generally showed his love to people of all sorts. While mission should also include a wide variety of other ministries in working for the kingdom of God, the central calling of Christian mission must, however, remain the preaching of forgiveness and salvation.

In his life Jesus set an example of prayerfulness in close union with his Father. John devotes a whole chapter – chapter 17 – to Jesus' prayer. Both the fact of his prayerfulness and the actual content of his prayer in chapter 17 challenge us as Christian workers in our calling to mission.

Jesus' prayer starts with the urgent request that the Father would glorify the Son, so that Jesus might be able to glorify the Father (17:1). In this context of glorifying the Son and the Father, Jesus' prayer underlines his ministry on earth. But now Jesus knows that he will return to the Father and his mission of salvation to the world will be carried forward by his followers. He prays for them that they may be kept safe even in the midst of persecution, that they should be sanctified even when living and working in the sinful context of a fallen world. And he prays that they may reflect the glorious unity of the Son with the Father in a godly oneness. Although the Father and the Son are distinct persons, they are fully one. Likewise, Christians retain their different characters and personalities but are called to manifest our unity as sisters and brothers in the one body of Christ.

We have already seen how Jesus was sent to identify with humanity and to become a first-century Jew with particular parents, culture, education and background. And yet, despite his absolute identification with the culture of his time and people, he remained uncompromisingly sinless. In its missionary calling the Christian Church is called also to relate culturally to the modern generation and yet to discern what in that culture is contrary to Christian holiness. We are aware of the danger of Christians living in a cultural ghetto, alien to those outside the Church. In cross-cultural mission too, workers are needed who will be willing to identify in their lifestyle, in their ways of thinking and communication. This will require considerable personal sacrifice. It will also necessitate years of being deeply immersed in the life and culture of the people to whom we are called. Short-term mission may have its uses, but in just a year or two it is impossible to attain such Christ-like cultural identification.

Theologians commonly underline the New Testament emphasis on Jesus as the suffering servant. Isaiah 53 was evidently prominent in the thinking of the first-century Church. Jesus gave the model of following a life of poverty and hardship in which he 'did not come to be served, but to serve, and to give his life . . .' (Mark 10:45). Christians are called to be sent in just the same way that he was sent by the Father, to walk in his footsteps as suffering servants.

It is easy to fall into the trap of developing proud status hierarchies in the Church or in missions, but this goes against the teaching and the example of Jesus. Slaves and servants in the first century had no rights over their lives and certainly could not lord it over others. Their total purpose was to serve their master and do his bidding. Likewise we are called to be servants of the Lord himself and so to be obedient to him. But we are also called to serve each other in humility and to serve our neighbour in the wider world, so church leaders are called 'ministers', which carries the sense of serving and has no sense of the dignity or status attached to that word today. In international mission, too, workers are needed who will work under the national churches, serving their needs and doing what the local leaders require. Likewise, we have to ask what the country we serve really needs. Unfortunately we have to admit that too many overseas workers insist on fulfilling the ministry they themselves feel called to and often yield to the temptation to build their own little empires. Pride can so easily afflict Christian workers.

It is noteworthy that the resurrection of Jesus with this final mission commission of 20:21 leads directly into the final chapter of John's Gospel. Here the resurrected Jesus enables his disciples miraculously to catch fish (21:1–14). By themselves they had been unable to catch even one fish all night, but with Jesus a miraculous haul of 153 fish threatened to break their nets. By means of a highly fanciful and subtle playing with numbers the old Anglo-Saxon bishop Alcuin (735–804) interpreted the number 153 to mean that the gospel must be preached to all peoples in all four corners of the world! While Alcuin's method of interpreting the number 153 is far-fetched, he nevertheless arrived at the right conclusion. This story does remind Jesus' disciples of their calling to be the Lord's instruments in fishing for all men and women everywhere. With this unforgettable visible sign, Jesus repeated the previous verbal teaching that for fruitful mission his followers need the presence of Jesus in the power of the Holy Spirit.

And finally the Gospel concludes with the reinstatement of Peter after his threefold denial of the Lord. Just as Peter had denied the Lord, so too all the disciples had failed him in his hour of critical need at his trial and crucifixion. Now Peter received the forgiveness of his Lord as the leader and representative of the whole body of the disciples. As Jesus gently led Peter into the experience of deep forgiveness and renewal, he recommissioned him to feed and take care of his sheep. So Peter's forgiveness leads directly into pastoral care of Jesus' Church and the wider task of feeding the world's crowds. Now the baton passes from Peter and the first disciples to us.

6

Romans – Paul,
apostle to the Gentiles:
chapters 1 to 8

'Romans is the most important book in the Bible,' declared the New York pastor as he introduced a new sermon series on Paul's letter to the Romans. While we may query whether God gives such priority to one biblical book over another, it is certainly true that Romans has played a central role in determining the beliefs of Christians through the ages. We shall therefore concentrate on Romans in these next chapters rather than examining all Paul's letters, which would certainly merit a whole volume on its own. Just to look at Romans in merely two chapters is already a challenge!

In order to understand Romans it is necessary to be aware of the situation in which it was written and to be aware of some of the questions facing Paul himself as he wrote the letter.

The background and purpose of the epistle

The church in Rome

The Roman historian Suetonius says in his *Life of Claudius* that the Roman emperor 'expelled the Jews from Rome because they were constantly rioting at the instigation of Chrestus'. Scholars agree that 'Chrestus' must here refer to 'Christ', which implies that there were Christians in Rome very early on in the history of the Church. The date of this expulsion was probably *c*. 49 AD, and it is mentioned in Acts 18:2 where Aquila and Priscilla are said to have recently arrived in Corinth from Rome. But by the time Romans was written they had returned to Rome (16:3). What does this expulsion and travel imply for the church in Rome?

It is evident from Paul's letter that he himself had not founded the church in Rome. It probably developed from the conversion of Jewish pilgrims from Rome to Jerusalem at Pentecost (Acts 2:10) who then returned to Rome with the good news of Jesus Christ. Not only Jews, but also Gentile proselytes (those who accepted the Jewish Law and were circumcised) and God-fearers (who did not accept the Law and were not circumcised) would soon have been added to the Church. They in turn would have led others to faith in Jesus Christ. Thus this church became a mixed Jew–Gentile community until the Jews were expelled and the Roman church became entirely Gentile.

Some years later some of the Jewish Christians, like Aquila and Priscilla, were able to return to Rome. Romans 14 and 15 show that this led to considerable problems. It seems that the Gentile house churches were less than enthusiastic in welcoming their Jewish brothers and sisters back. Likewise, the Jewish believers found it hard to relate to Gentile Christians who did not follow the prescribed Jewish laws on Sabbath and clean or unclean foods. So Paul writes to encourage both sets of house churches towards loving unity in Christ.

Paul is evidently writing this letter with the situation in Rome very much in mind. Although he did not plant the church in

Rome and therefore felt he did not have the right to teach with authority, he nevertheless wants to strengthen the church in its particular needs. Paul's heart lay in his calling to pioneer church planting (15:20), but he nevertheless wrote his epistles in order to teach and build up the churches. This ministry within the Church of God is surely a vital element in Christian mission. Church planting alone is not sufficient without further teaching and growth in Christian holiness.

Mission to Spain

Paul's heart for the worldwide spread of the gospel was constantly impelling him forwards to new frontiers for Christ. It is clear from 15:24 and 28 that Paul's purpose in visiting Rome was with a view to wider mission to Spain. He evidently wanted the Roman church to be a launching pad for his new pioneer outreach. Because he valued their support and prayer it was incumbent upon him to justify his calling as God's chosen apostle to the Gentiles and thus to demonstrate that mission to Gentiles is a valid calling. Most probably many of the Gentiles in the Roman church were already associated with Israel. They were almost certainly very largely circumcised proselytes or at least 'God-fearers' who had previously joined themselves to the Jewish synagogue but had not fully submitted to the Jewish Law and been circumcised. In either case they were no longer purely Gentile.

But in his desire to evangelise Spain, Paul was posing a new question. Is it right to evangelise pure Gentiles who are in no way part of Israel? Or is the Jewish Messiah only for his own Jewish people and for those Gentiles who have already been joined to the people of Israel? The answer to this vital question would become the foundation for the universality of the Christian Church and the basis for international mission.

In the first century, people did not divide the world into continents – Africa, Europe, Asia, etc. They pictured the world in concentric circles. The centre of the earth was the Mediterranean Sea. Its very name, *medi-terra* (meaning 'middle of the earth') shows this. All around the Mediterranean lay the 'civilised world' – North Africa, western Asia, southern Europe. Then came the wider circle of the 'barbarians' in black Africa, central and northern Europe, plus the vast territories of Asia beyond the Middle East. According to tradition Peter concentrated largely on evangelism in the Middle East while Mark went down to Egypt as the gateway to North Africa. Thomas is the only one known to us to have ventured beyond the 'civilised world' in journeying far away to India and planting the Church there. Paul himself was called to evangelise the northern coast of the Mediterranean. By the time he wrote this letter he had founded strong churches in the area between Jerusalem and modern-day Albania and Bosnia (15:19) which would take the gospel out beyond the cities into the villages and thus fulfil the task of evangelising the whole of that region. Now he wanted to move on to the extreme end of the 'civilised world' and evangelise beyond Rome, even to Spain in the far west. So in his letter to the Roman Christians he needed to convince them of the rightness of his calling and thus persuade them to support him in his mission.

Paul's purpose in this letter relates closely to modern mission. Many in the Church today need to be persuaded that it is right to take the Christian gospel to different peoples with different religious backgrounds all over the world. Only when they have embraced this challenge will they support mission workers in their task of evangelism and church planting.

Church leaders in Jerusalem

In chapter 15 Paul highlights a further purpose in writing to the church in Rome. He is evidently about to go to Jerusalem to take them a gift from the Gentile churches in Macedonia and Achaia (15:26, 27). But Paul is uncertain just how he will be received in Jerusalem (15:31). Coming from his background as a well-known leading Jew and yet mixing so freely with Gentiles, how will he be viewed by non-Christian Jews in Jerusalem? Will they stir up fierce persecution or throw him out of the city? He is also nervous of his reception by the Christian Jewish leadership in the mother church of Jerusalem. Will they accept a gift from Gentile churches and thus put their stamp of approval on Paul's Gentile ministry? Or will they reject him and the Gentiles' gift? If so, radical division will come into the Church. Paul's apostolic ministry will then lose its validity in the eyes of other Christians because it will lack acceptance from Jerusalem, the foundational church which was held in tremendous esteem.

The Gentile churches' gift to the Christians in Jerusalem not only had the aim of alleviating their poverty, but also represented a token of the Gentiles' debt to the Jews for the gift of the gospel of the Messiah. In addition it demonstrated a sense of Gentile Christian solidarity with Jewish Christians which was important for the mixed Jew–Gentile church in Rome itself. Perhaps, too, Paul had Isaiah 60:5 in mind and saw this gift as a fulfilment of the prophecy that the wealth of the nations/Gentiles would come to Zion.

But there was a real possibility that Jewish Christians in both Jerusalem and Rome might object to the gift because it showed an acceptance of Paul's gospel of grace and salvation without the Law. And the Gentile Christians in Rome might also be suspicious of Paul's collection because it seemed to tie them to Jerusalem and their Jewish roots.

For his Jewish readers, therefore, Paul needed to demonstrate in his epistle that he still maintained his Jewish roots despite his emphasis on mission to Gentiles. He writes against all accusations that he neglected the Jewish Law and so was morally lax and unrighteous. Likewise, he is careful to show that he still honours God's covenant with Israel through Moses. Paul demonstrates that God still has definite purposes of mercy towards his chosen people, Israel.

Paul's positive approach towards the Mosaic Law and God's plan for Israel is of vital importance for Jewish Christians today. It reminds Gentile Christians too that they should not neglect the Jewish roots of the Christian Church. It is so easy for Gentile churches to concentrate on the later traditions and teachings of the Church with little thought of the Jewish foundations of the New Testament and the Christian Church.

Paul's emphasis on righteousness in this epistle also challenges the Christian Church to remember that moral holiness is essential for all worshippers of the God of holiness. While it remains true that we are justified by faith alone and not by our good works or merit, we dare not separate justification from its necessary fruit of righteousness. The Christian emphasis on God's grace must not lead to a neglect of godly living and holiness in submission to the law of Christ.

A theological treatise?

Particularly since the Reformation, the doctrine of justification by faith alone has been central to evangelical theology, as also to the Christian life. Romans has been particularly influential as the foundation for this doctrine. It was in the study of this letter that Luther himself found new life and freedom. Scholars and ordinary Christians alike have walked in Luther's footsteps, finding the reality of God's life-changing grace through the reading of Paul's letter to the Romans. As a result, many have felt that this epistle declares Paul's theology, and they see it as fundamentally a theological treatise.

In its extreme, this view of Romans almost parallels this letter with a systematic theology book and has no apparent reference to the existential situation of Paul himself or the Roman church to which he was writing. Other more moderate proponents of this view still see Romans as a carefully argued declaration of Paul's theology, but they also note that he is outlining his theology in the context of his and the Roman church's particular situations.

But it should be noted that nowhere else does Paul or any other New Testament writer give an existentially unrelated theological exposition. While their theology may indeed be based on the objective content of God's revelation, all theological expositions in the New Testament are related to the particular situations and needs of the church to which they are speaking.

Revelation is God's objective word to humanity, but theology is merely the human attempt to understand that revelation and formulate its content. It may therefore be fairly said that unrelated theological teaching is unbiblical. All theology must be contextual, even though it stems from objective revelation.

Actually, however, Paul's letter to the Romans is hardly an adequate exposition of theology. In this letter Paul fails to give detailed teaching on some essential areas of the Christian faith. For example, there is no parallel to his careful and detailed exposition of the incarnation such as he gives us in Philippians 2. And although Paul refers frequently to our future hope in glory throughout this epistle, he does not give any teaching equivalent to 1 Corinthians 15 on the resurrection or to 1 Thessalonians on the second coming of Jesus.

But in chapters 1 to 4 Paul does outline his fundamental teaching on sin and justification by faith in the atoning work of Christ on the cross. He then proceeds to give further detailed exposition of his theology of sin in chapter 6, of the Law in chapter 7, and of life in the Holy Spirit in chapter 8. These chapters clearly teach the reality of our union with Christ in his death, resurrection and glorification. As we were in Adam and therefore have come under sin and death, so now we are in Christ and have received his gift of life. But all of these theological discourses are in the specific context of Paul's desire that the Roman church support his Gentile mission to Spain, and his anxiety concerning his visit to Jerusalem and the fathers of the church there.

Anti-Judaisers

Commentators point out that Paul's epistle to the Romans was almost certainly written soon after his heated encounter with Judaisers in Galatia and Corinth. They had sought to undermine his ministry among the Gentiles by declaring that all believers in Jesus must be circumcised and follow the Jewish Law. Although Gentile believers in the God of Israel in Old Testament times had been required to join themselves to the people of Israel in that way, Paul saw that Jesus was widening the kingdom to include Gentiles as Gentiles. No longer did they need to become little Jews in order to follow the Jewish Messiah. Paul underlined the universality of the gospel – a foundational truth for the Church throughout all ages. As fellow-workers with Christ we are called to share his vision for all peoples everywhere. And Christians do not have to conform to one particular ethnic model. Just as the early Gentile Christians did not have to lose their Gentile cultural background, so also Christians today are not required to adopt American, European or Korean religious forms. The Christian gospel fits into every culture.

Having noted briefly the background and purpose of the epistle, we need now to examine the actual text of the letter.

The introduction – Paul's apostleship (1:1–15)

Paul declares his position right in the very first words. He is called by God to serve Jesus Christ as an apostle among all nations (1:1–6). While both RSV and NIV call Paul a 'servant' of Jesus Christ, the Greek word actually means a slave. Although slavery was at that time a bitter and widespread practice, Paul does not hesitate to use this demeaning term for himself. He willingly became a slave with no personal rights whose whole purpose in life was joyfully to serve his master. He thus acknowledges Jesus' total lordship over everything in his life.

In his position as a slave of Christ, Paul was called to be an apostle, one who was sent by God with a mission. It was not by his own choice or desire that Paul decided to preach to the Gentiles of all nations. This was entirely God's call. It was God who 'set [him] apart for the gospel of God' (1:1). As Christians, our lives are at God's disposal, and for each one of us it is our responsibility to ask God what he wants us to do and where he wants us to serve him.

God's purpose for Paul was that he should be dedicated to the spread of the good news of Jesus Christ among all nations.

The word used for 'nations' refers particularly to the Gentiles, so Paul is claiming right at the very beginning of his letter that God has sent him to bring the gospel not only to his own people but also to the Gentiles. His message is based on the resurrection of Jesus Christ, designated Son of God in power by the Spirit of holiness. This combination of power and holiness is significant. And his aim is that the Gentiles might come to the quality of faith which produces obedience to the Lord (1:5).

Paul's international vision is further demonstrated in 1:8–15. In his thanksgiving for them, the one thing he picks out in the life and faith of the Roman Christians is that their faith is 'reported all over the world'. And he concludes these verses by stating his obligation to all peoples (1:14), which underlies his desire to come to Rome and preach the gospel there.

These initial verses make it abundantly clear that Paul's overriding purpose in this letter is the fulfilment of his apostolic call to preach the gospel to the Gentiles. Everything else is subordinate to this great international mission vision.

The foundation text (1:16, 17)

It is generally recognised that 1:16–17 forms the text which is then expounded and developed in the rest of this letter. Paul's fundamental assertion rings out with absolute confidence – he is not ashamed of the gospel. Indeed, these words could be turned into the positive statement that Paul's sure faith in the good news of Jesus Christ undergirds his whole life and ministry. Jesus Christ is the very centre of Paul's thinking.

Paul's assured confidence is based on the fact that the gospel demonstrates God's power in action, bringing the glories of salvation both to Jews and to Gentiles of every nation. 'To the Jew and also the Gentile' will become a common refrain in this letter and marks the primary purpose of Paul's letter to the Romans. The universality of the gospel is central to his message.

Paul gives a particular twist to his affirmation of the universal nature of the gospel of Jesus. He states that it is 'first for the Jew'.

The NIV translators evidently understood the word 'first' in its temporal sense, so they add 'then' for the Gentiles. As we have seen, it was of course true that the gospel was preached first to Jews and only later to Gentiles. But by the time Romans was written this fact was so obvious that it was quite unnecessary to point it out. And such a statement added nothing to what the Roman Christians already believed. It is much more likely that the phrase 'first for the Jew' has a sense of priority. Paul is saying that God has a particular concern and loving purpose for the Jews as his covenant people. In the church in Rome, Gentile believers probably outnumbered their Jewish sisters and brothers, so they could easily look down on them with arrogant pride. Paul therefore reminds his readers that God still gives priority to his people Israel. But in the same breath he also affirms that the gospel is not only for Jews, but equally for Gentiles. This tension of the priority of the Jews and yet the equality of Jew and Gentile is constantly present in Romans.

As he will develop in the following chapters, the good news of Jesus Christ is then both for Jews and Gentiles equally because it is the means of righteousness through faith, not through the works of the Jewish Law. The twin topics of righteousness and faith run like a thread through the whole material of Romans – and the Law of Moses joins them as a major theme in this epistle.

In 1:17 Paul quotes from Habakkuk 2:4, but slightly changes the significance of Habakkuk's words. In Habakkuk the prophet is bewildered by God's declaration that he will use the utterly idolatrous and evil Chaldeans as his instrument to judge Israel, the people of God. How can an utterly holy God employ such an evil and treacherous nation to 'swallow up those more righteous than themselves' (Hab. 1:13)? Habakkuk therefore waits for God to reveal his answer to the prophet's problems. He determines to wait patiently for God's answer. And it is in this context that the word comes that 'the righteous shall live by their faith'. Here the word 'faith' clearly refers to patient faithfulness rather than a specific act of faith.

In Hebrews 10:38 the Habakkuk verse is used to support the need for ongoing faithfulness rather than an act of faith. In Hebrews 11 the writer lists a variety of great heroes who have faithfully persevered despite extreme suffering. The aim is to encourage the letter's readers not to 'shrink back' or 'throw away their confidence' by turning away from the Lord, but rather to press on with faithfulness and endurance.

In Galatians 3:11, however, Habakkuk 2:4 is used to underline the fact that we are justified by our turning to Jesus in faith, not by the Law. Likewise in Romans 1:17 it refers to the placing of our faith in Jesus Christ as the means of salvation and righteousness. Of course, the initial act of putting one's faith in Jesus Christ must lead to a life of ongoing faithfulness, so that faith and faithfulness always go hand in hand together. But while Habakkuk and Hebrews are thinking more of ongoing faithfulness, Romans and Galatians relate more to the foundational attitude of faith in Christ.

Both initial faith and persevering faithfulness are essential in the life of the Christian Church. Without the initial act of putting one's trust in Christ there can be no development of righteousness. In addition, the New Testament warns Christians of the trials of suffering and persecution. Particularly in such circumstances, ongoing faithfulness and patient endurance will shine like a beacon in the darkness.

Sin is the universal problem (1:18–3:20)

The salvation of which Paul speaks in 1:16 is not only positively unto righteousness, but also negatively from sin. He will develop the theme of righteousness more fully in chapters 5 to 8, but now he proceeds to demonstrate that all peoples everywhere are under sin and need salvation.

The universality of sin has been a politically incorrect assertion already for centuries in the western world. Romantic philosophers like Rousseau after the French Revolution maintained a naïve view of the 'pure native' who was born without sin and lived the idyllic life of perfect purity. When John Wesley went initially as a missionary to North America, even he thought that he would see in the American Indians the perfect Christian life without the deleterious influences of decadent Europe. He was sadly disillusioned to find that the Indians and their way of life were also far from ideal. Now, in the twenty-first century, Europeans tend to think of African and eastern societies as ideally beautiful, and it is considered unacceptable to see negatives in these overseas cultures.

Having lived ourselves in a variety of east Asian cultures among people of all the various Asian religions, we have seen both good and evil. In some areas of life we felt strongly that we as Europeans could learn much from our Asian friends, but we also noted serious cultural weaknesses and personal sin. Paul, too, in Romans, is very realistic and honest. He observes that all people and all peoples are under the dominion of sin. This basic truth underlies the call of Christians to go into all the world to preach the good news of salvation through Jesus Christ.

Paul starts in 1:18–32 by showing that the Gentiles are sinners. Their sin is partly religious, with the practice of idolatry and the worship of the created rather than the Creator. Of course, the created can take many forms. It may be actual wooden idols or it may be less tangible forms of idolatry. Recently in Britain posters adorned motorway service stations with the message that 'Football is our religion'!

But Gentile sin is also moral, and Paul lists the shockingly evil consequences of a society without Jesus Christ at the centre (1:26–31). The modern reader may be shocked by the way Paul places homosexuality alongside murder – and these are accompanied by such sins as gossip, greed, strife, arrogance and disobedience to parents. So sins that really shock us stand alongside sins which are accepted as normal in everyday life. But all such sins lead to cultural disintegration and the breakdown of society, as well as personal unhappiness and insecurity. As we survey Paul's tragic list of Gentile sins, we can only long for the salvation and new life which Jesus came to bring us. What a clarion call to mission!

It is noteworthy that Paul links moral sin to religious sin. They go together. False worship will inevitably lead to ethical disorder. The Bible strongly underlines the holiness of God and therefore the absolute demand that those who worship the holy God should themselves be holy. Jews and Christians will therefore have been shocked to read that some of the hijackers who destroyed the World Trade Center in September 2001 rented hard-core pornographic videos for their last night before they committed suicide and faced the judgment. They were fanatics in their religion, but they evidently had little sense of a holy God demanding holiness in his people. Likewise, in modern western forms of New Age and Paganism, their followers can be very 'spiritual' and yet quite immoral. Of course, Christians too fall into moral sin, but this contradicts their profession.

With centuries of Christian influence in the west, non-Christians sometimes delight to point the finger if they can catch a Christian in moral inconsistency. 'I thought you called yourself a Christian,' they may say accusingly. Little do they realise that it is through biblical teaching that they link religious faith with ethical holiness. This connection of religion and ethics needs to be stressed in Christian teaching, not only in countries with little Christian influence in their history but also increasingly in today's Europe and America.

Having shown the fearful sinfulness of the Gentiles, Paul now widens his argument to include anyone who 'passes judgment on someone else' (2:1). This verse makes it clear that Paul is no longer outlining Gentile sin only, but that his attention has now turned to all people. When Paul was describing Gentile sin, his Jewish readers might well have nodded their heads in smug agreement. But the finger of accusation is coming closer! Paul's methodology is reminiscent of the prophet Amos, who starts by declaring God's judgment on the sins of Israel's surrounding nations before turning to the sin of Israel herself. So Israel's applause dies down and is replaced by anger – or, hopefully, by repentance.

In 2:17, therefore, Paul turns specifically to the sin of the Jews who 'brag' that they are God's chosen people possessing God's Law and covenant. They rely on the Law as the guarantee of their relationship with God (2:17). As people of the covenant they feel confident of God's grace. Paul declares that, as the outward sign of this covenant, circumcision 'has value if you observe the law', but if you break God's commands you 'become as though you had not been circumcised' (2:25). It is circumcision of the heart by the Holy Spirit which brings life (2:28, 29). Sadly, however, the majority of Israel's people have surrendered to the power of sin in their lives.

So Paul summarises this first section of his epistle by making the foundational statement that 'Jews and Gentiles alike are all under sin' (3:9). This foundational statement is so important and perhaps also so controversial that he backs it up with a long list of Old Testament quotations (3:10–18). The rabbis call this 'pearl-stringing'. What a model for Christians that we should support our arguments with sound biblical teaching! By the end of verse 18, his readers will have held up their hands in holy surrender and agreement.

Paul summarises this section by declaring that God's law is not intended to bring the justifying righteousness of salvation, for all people fail and break the law. The law does however make us aware of our sin as we stand accountable before God (3:19, 20).

God's solution to the problem of sin (3:21–4:25)

Good doctors not only diagnose but also propose suitable remedies for the patient's illness. Paul has diagnosed the universal problem of sin. Now he outlines the remedy.

In 3:21–6 he gives a tight-knit argument concerning how people may attain God's righteousness 'apart from law' and declares that this is nothing new. The Old Testament Scriptures in the Law and the Prophets have already testified to this. The answer is faith in Jesus Christ for all people who will believe (3:22). All people of every race have sinned and still all the time fall short of God's perfect standards of glory. Paul then uses a series of vital theological terms: 'justify', 'grace', 'redemption', 'propitiation'/'sacrifice of atonement'. Our salvation may be seen from God's perspective, in which his wrath against sin is propitiated by the sacrifice of his Son Jesus Christ. It may also be viewed from a human angle, in which our sin is cleansed and we are justified and accounted righteous. In either case, we as sinners are reconciled to the all-holy God through faith in Christ and his sacrificial death on our behalf.

The word 'justified' has been interpreted in different ways. Traditionally, Roman Catholics noted the Latin which literally means 'to make just'. Protestants went back to the original Greek which means 'to reckon as just'. So Roman Catholics emphasised the need for ongoing sanctification whereby we strive to become holy and move towards the goal of righteousness and future salvation. Protestants, on the other hand, noted that because of the shed blood of Jesus on the cross God imputes to us his righteousness, while Jesus takes our sin upon himself (e.g. 2 Cor. 5:21). Protestants therefore can have a greater assurance of their salvation, which has already been given to us through the imputed righteousness of Christ. This Protestant view fits the thought of Paul, who rejoiced in the unmerited grace of God in covering sinful people with the perfect righteousness of Christ. Paul would have loved the old expression 'sinners saved by grace'.

So the means of our salvation from sin are clear. Jesus' sacrificial death on our behalf pays the penalty for sin and deals also with the wrath of God. Thus God can be reconciled with sinners, and a new relationship with God is forged. The question still remains, however: is the atoning death of the Jewish Messiah only valid for his own people, the Jews? Or is it also for Gentiles? Is Jesus Christ the means of salvation for all peoples equally?

In the final verses of Romans 3 Paul shows that justification does not come through the works of the Law, but by faith in

Jesus Christ. If salvation depended on the Jewish Law, it would of course be only for Jews – and those Gentiles who joined themselves to the people of Israel by becoming proselytes, being circumcised and following the Law of Moses. If this were the case, the Christian Church would be merely a messianic sect of Judaism, not a universal faith for all peoples equally. But Paul states categorically that justification is by faith in Jesus Christ – and all people of whatever background can come to put their faith in Jesus.

In his commentary on Romans, Luther had problems understanding why 3:29 follows logically after 3:28. Why does justification by faith apart from works of Law lead on to the questions: 'Is God the God of Jews only? Is he not the God of Gentiles too?' If Paul had been talking about faith versus works in general, then the sequence of the verses seems illogical. But if Paul is talking of works *of the Jewish Law*, then verse 29 follows naturally.

Paul further underlines the truth that God and his salvation are for Gentiles as well as Jews by quoting the *Shema*, the creed of Israel: 'God is one.' Traditionally the rabbis have always understood this word to mean that God is the only Lord and therefore he is God of all peoples everywhere. God is unique and all other deities are mere idols. All peoples ought to worship the one true God.

Throughout history, Jews have boasted in their possession of the Law. They are the chosen people of the covenant who are unique in having the Torah, the Law of Moses. This relationship with God has been thought to depend on the Law. And, of course, people under the Law want to be obedient and do the works of the Law. Thus the Law can lead to pride and the danger of seeking merit through doing good works.

So Paul picks up on the idea of 'boasting' (3:27; 4:2) to show that we would have something to boast about if our justification was the reward for our good works. This concept may be interpreted generally of all works of merit, as the Reformers understood Paul's theology. But it is more in tune with his teaching to link 'works' to the Jewish Law. It is not just a question of works versus faith but of works of the Jewish Law versus faith. This fits the whole context of Romans 4, which again underlines the universality of the Christian faith. Abraham is 'the father of *many nations*', not just of Israel (4:17, 18), 'the father of us *all*' (4:16), 'the father of *all* who believe' (4:11).

Although Paul characteristically avoids all denigration of the Law and stresses that he is not 'nullifying' it, he is showing that the Jewish Law is not God's means of salvation. To prove this to his Jewish readers he uses the example of Abraham. If it is true for 'our father Abraham', it will be convincing for all Jews.

Paul proves that justification and God's gift of imputed righteousness are not through the Law by pointing out that Abraham was justified *before* he was circumcised (4:9–12). Circumcision was the visible outward sign of being under the Law. He adds that it was not through the Mosaic Law that Abraham received the promise that he would be heir to the world, but through the righteousness that comes by faith. In parallel fashion, Galatians shows that Abraham was justified 430 years before the giving of the Law on Mount Sinai. The contrast is justification by faith as opposed to justification by the Law. It is not justification by faith rather than by good works, as the Reformers emphasised. There were of course plenty of good works before the time of Abraham! So it is nonsense to say that Abraham was justified by faith, not by good works, because he was justified before good works existed! Abraham was, however, justified by faith long before God gave Israel the Mosaic Law.

As we have already noted, if justification were through the works of the Jewish Law, it would be for Jews only. But happily we are justified by God's grace through faith alone, so God's wonderful gift is open to all who will believe in Jesus Christ. By his death all believers have been delivered from their sins, and by his resurrection God brings all believers into new life (4:25). The universal problem of sin has indeed a universally available solution in the atoning work of Jesus Christ's death and resurrection, which may be appropriated by God's grace and through faith alone.

If God justifies all nations equally, the Church has the supreme responsibility to share that good news worldwide.

Paul elaborates on the glories of our salvation (chapters 5 to 8)

In these chapters Paul waxes eloquent in developing some of the themes briefly mentioned in the first four chapters. He rejoices in our justification from sin and death by the grace and love of God through the shed blood and sacrificial death of Jesus Christ. The gift of righteousness apart from Law for all people is highlighted. And he looks forward to the Christian's hope in glory and the perfection of our future final salvation.

All these themes are developed in chapter 5, which forms a bridge between the first four chapters and the following three. Some commentators have therefore linked chapter 5 with the first chapters, while others have bracketed it with the ensuing three.

In 5:1–11, Paul outlines some of the fruits of the justification of which he has spoken particularly in chapter 3. Christians need to be taught not only how they are justified by grace through faith without having to submit to the Law, but also the glorious inheritance into which that justification leads us. 'Peace with God' heads the list. In 3:25 Paul has already mentioned the 'sacrifice of atonement' which we have through the shed blood of Jesus. The word is much debated, but it means that the wrath of God against our sin is stilled. The burning anger and judgment of our all-holy God no longer hangs over us because Jesus has paid the price for our sins and has died for us. As a result, Paul now declares, we have peace with God. We are reconciled to him and can now enjoy an unclouded relationship of love with him. His love has broken through the thick cloud of our sin and we can now ascend into the sunshine of peace with him.

As a result of that peace with God, we have direct access into his presence (5:2). Some years ago a neighbour of ours constantly boasted that she had a friend who was a millionaire. Eventually

I countered this by telling her that I too had a millionaire friend, but mine never leaves me alone and is always with me! We have direct access to him at all times. And Paul goes on to affirm that we look forward with confident hope to sharing God's glory perfectly. We rejoice in the present, but look forward eagerly too to the future glory.

But Paul is realistic. The Christian life is not all milk and honey. Suffering is a very real part of Christian discipleship. This was not only true of the first century, but remains so right through history even to our time. Horrendous stories of persecution and suffering have marred the twentieth century, and already in our present century it seems to gather pace. Fearful suffering comes upon Christians in Muslim countries, drought and famine affect Christians and non-Christians alike in Africa and elsewhere, poverty and injustice grind Christians down in Latin American and other mega-cities and in rural communities. But Paul is positive even about such sufferings (5:3–5) – and he was speaking from personal experience. He even talks of 'rejoicing' in our suffering, which in the modern west European context sounds naïvely counter-cultural. With prosperity and comfort-zones to the forefront, Christians are ill prepared to rejoice in suffering. But Paul is deeply aware that suffering works into our lives the virtue of persevering endurance. This in turn produces 'character', a word which signifies experience which has been tested and proved. And such tested experience now undergirds the sure hope Christians have of the promised future glory. Our experience and hope are shown even now to be trustworthy because we already enjoy the work of the Holy Spirit pouring God's love into our hearts (5:5). As in the book of Acts, the sure proof of God's grace is found in the outpoured gift of the Holy Spirit.

Having reiterated the fact that all God's grace results from the death of Christ for sinners (5:6–8), Paul comes back to the words of 5:1 (5:8). Our present justification guarantees our ultimate future salvation from God's wrath. Again, the present fact of our reconciliation with God prefigures our future full salvation.

All the glorious benefits of God's grace and Christ's sacrificial death are available for 'all people' (5:12, 18), for 'the many' (5:15, 19). Just as sin presents a universal problem, so likewise salvation is freely available for all people and all peoples.

Chapter 6 picks up on the theme of 'life' (5:21). While chapter 5 concentrated on the death of Christ, chapter 6 majors on the resurrection which brings new life to God's people. In contrast to sin and death, Christ was raised so that we too might 'live a new life' (6:4). We have died with Christ and now we can live his resurrected life. So Paul exhorts us to 'count ourselves dead to sin'. As a corpse no longer hears anything, so we are no longer to hear the voice of sin. Rather, we are to live in oneness with God and for the Lord (6:11). Sin should no longer dominate us, for we are no longer ruled by the Law and its demands. Grace now holds sway in our lives and motivates all we are and all we do. Paul is well aware of the possible accusation that being no longer under Law might be thought to allow Christians to sin freely (6:15). Indeed, he has already countered the suggestion that we might continue in sin so that grace might flourish more (6:1–4). Paul therefore states that we have been freed from slavery to sin and have become 'slaves to righteousness' and 'slaves to God'. Paul is more concerned with the new life of righteousness than with demands for freedom.

In chapter 7 Paul confronts the hot topic of the Mosaic Law. While Jews boasted in the Law and some Jewish Christians even exalted the Law as God's means of election and salvation, Paul has already shown that justification and salvation come only by grace and through the atoning death of Jesus. He begins his discussion of the Law by proving that it is no longer binding on us because we are one with Jesus in his death. As death terminates a marriage union, so likewise it terminates our union with the Law and its consequent sin and death. Paul notes that it is through the Law that we become aware of sin and fall under its sway. Through the Law we 'know' sin in that deep biblical sense of a mystical union and intimate relationship. But now we 'know' God through Jesus Christ.

Jewish critics might attack Paul for this apparent denigration of God's Law. Throughout Romans, Paul imagines critical questions against his teaching. Using the interesting device of an imaginary heckler, Paul handles the inevitable Jewish objection that he appears to denigrate God's Law: 'What shall we say then? Is the Law sin?' Strongly rejecting such a suggestion, he explains that he would not have known what sin is except through the Law (7:7). He is by no means against the Law. Indeed, he reaffirms that the Law and its commandments are 'holy, righteous and good'.

But still he faces a problem. 'Did that which is good, then, become death to me?' No, it was sin, not the Law, which brought death. So he observes the struggle between carnal human nature and 'the desire to do what is good'. Commentators disagree whether Paul is describing his own personal struggles before or after his regeneration, or whether he is describing the inner battles which rage in all believers' lives or only in the heart of the unbeliever. However, the repeated 'I' and 'me' would seem to indicate that the battle of righteousness against Law, sin and death was his own personal experience. Christians would testify with Paul that we all face the same struggle. Muslims too are aware of the inner *jihad* struggle against our evil inclinations. But Paul finally exults in what Muslims can know nothing of, namely the reality of victory and deliverance through Jesus Christ who is our Lord.

Paul's ultimate purpose in describing his inner struggle is to show that the Law of God is positive and still to be served. This contrasts with 'the law of sin' (7:25).

And so Paul comes to the climax of this section in Chapter 8. Here he declares the very heart of the glorious message we proclaim to the world. Once again everything is based on the sacrificial death and life-giving resurrection of Jesus, with whom Christians enjoy an unbreakable relationship. But in this chapter Paul picks up on what he has previously stated in 5:5 and 7:6, for it is by the Holy Spirit that the benefits of our salvation come to us. It is through the Holy Spirit which has been poured into our hearts that we experience God's love. And it is by the Holy Spirit that we are liberated from the dominion of the Law.

So what does Paul teach about the Holy Spirit in Romans 8? The Christian today is challenged to make sure that our teaching about the Spirit matches this biblical input. In verse 2 he immediately calls the Holy Spirit 'the Spirit of life', for it is through the Spirit that we are given life. Interestingly, this word concerning life is linked to the Spirit's dominion over us by the use of the word 'law'. And it is 'by the law of the Spirit of life' that God grants the gift of freedom from the dominion/law of sin and death, the two old enemies which Paul has described so vividly in the preceding chapters. As Christians walk according to the leading of the Spirit, they enjoy life and peace (8:4–6), pleasing God himself (8:8). What a privilege to be allowed to give pleasure to almighty God!

Thanks to the work of the Holy Spirit, slavery to fear is abolished and sinners are adopted as God's children (8:14–17) in such an intimate relationship that we can now call God *Abba*, the familiar term equivalent to 'Daddy'. And as his children Christians share with Christ in the Father's rich inheritance – what the Father possesses will pass on to his children. There are only two conditions for this close relationship as God's children and for inheriting all his grace. First, we must be prepared to 'share in his sufferings' and thus also 'in his glory' (8:17). In the kingdom of God there can be no glory without first suffering. The cross always precedes the glory of resurrection life.

The second condition for receiving the inheritance of God's children is that we are 'led by the Spirit of God' (8:14). Paul is talking here of a life which is under the direction of the Holy Spirit, following his commands. He has already declared that all Christians 'have the Spirit' and therefore the Spirit 'lives in you' (8:9–11), but now comes the question of whether the Christian is willing to be led by the Spirit. This is the antidote to sin, death and fear. It opens the door to sharing in the inheritance of Christ's resurrection life as children of the Father.

Again Paul is realistic. He knows that we do not yet

experience the fullness of our inheritance. So he underlines the word 'hope' by repeating it four times in verses 24 and 25. Just as the created order groans as it awaits its final regeneration, so the Spirit also groans in us. The Spirit within us expresses our longing and sure hope that God's glory will be revealed. The Spirit thus helps us in our weakness and prays within us according to the Father's will. Prayer can so easily degenerate into a 'shopping list' and we all often feel how impossible it is to put into words the depths of our longings. Some use the gift of tongues to express the inexpressible, others enjoy meditational silence before the Lord when the Spirit can do the speaking on our behalf.

In this passage Paul widens the horizons from his earlier emphasis on all peoples, Jews and Gentiles. Now he affirms that all creation will be renewed, reminding us of Colossians 1:15–20 with its repetition of 'all things'. The New Testament looks forward not only to a new humanity from all nations, but also to a renewed creation with a new heaven and new earth. Ecology is a vital part of Christian mission, and the message of a new creation with renewed beauty and order brings a smile of joy to the face of many in severely polluted areas of the world.

Paul concludes this section with the ringing endorsement of our relationship with Christ. Thanks to his death and resurrection, no one can bring any accusation against us. We are justified by his grace. His cross has paid the full price for our sin and brought us into union with the love of Christ. Absolutely nothing can separate us from the love of Christ. We live all the time in the confidence that Jesus Christ loves us and his love can never be removed from us. What a message for a lost and loveless world!

7

Romans – Paul,
apostle to the Gentiles:
chapters 9 to 16

Chapters 9 to 11: God's mercy to Jew and Gentile

For the sake of convenience we are dividing our section on Romans into two chapters. It would be too long for one chapter only. But Romans is actually like a seamless garment which does not really allow for any sharp division between one section and another. Chapters 9 to 11 clearly follow from the first eight chapters, and equally they lead directly into the concluding chapters of the letter. Some commentators have had problems in understanding how chapters 9 to 11 fit the context of the whole epistle and particularly the so-called 'doctrinal' section of the letter in chapters 1 to 8. But as we look at Romans 9 to 11 it will become obvious that chapters 1 to 8 would be gravely inadequate and incomplete if they did not lead on to chapters 9 to 11.

Paul summarises the argument of chapters 1 to 8 by declaring that nothing can 'separate us from the love of Christ' (8:35). In

9:3, however, he movingly declares that in his loving concern for his fellow Jews he could wish that he was 'cursed and cut off from Christ' (cf. Exod. 32:32). Verse 3 of chapter 9 follows naturally, therefore, from 8:35.

Likewise, in 11:30–2 Paul talks of God's mercies both to Jews and to Gentiles, which moves directly to 12:1. In accordance with God's mercies (RSV wording) he urges the Roman Christians to offer their bodies as living sacrifices. Some translations of 12:1 use a slightly different word for 'mercies', but it is synonymous with the word used in 11:30–2 and the change of word is merely a question of style. The context of offering our bodies as living sacrifices is therefore God's mercy to all people, both to Jews and Gentiles everywhere. The purpose for which we offer our bodies sacrificially is that God might pour out his mercies abundantly on the multitudes of all nations. So chapters 9 to 11 are inseparably tied in to the chapters which precede and follow them.

We have already observed that in chapters 1 to 8 Paul is underlining the universality of God's saving purposes in Christ. Jews and Gentiles are equally under sin. There is no difference between them in this fundamental problem. Equally, he declares, Gentiles and Jews receive salvation by the same means. Both are justified by faith in Jesus Christ, not by the works of the Law/ Torah. Inevitably now the question arises: what about God's particular purposes for Israel? Has God's covenant with Israel gone out of the window? Has Israel now lost its favour with God and been replaced by the Gentiles?

Romans 9 to 11 reveals Paul's struggle with these questions. His passionate concern for his own people and their salvation faces the sad reality that they have largely rejected Jesus as Messiah and Saviour. And in his particular love for his own Jewish people he does not want to compromise the truths that he has already expounded, namely that Jew and Gentile alike are under sin and find salvation equally through faith in Jesus Christ. In these three chapters, Paul asks various questions before finally arriving at his climactic vision of God's final mission statement for Jews and Gentiles in 11:11–32.

Of course it is wonderful to gain a clear view of God's great purposes for the world, but should Christians then merely twiddle their thumbs in passive prayer as they watch God unfold his plan? What responsibility do Christians bear in the out-working of God's mission? Chapters 12 to 15 develop Paul's answer to these questions.

So we need to look briefly at the questions Paul asks.

Has God's word failed? (9:1–13)

Having strongly affirmed his heartfelt anguish at Israel's rejection of Jesus Christ and his continued appreciation of their high calling and privilege as God's covenant people, Paul asks whether God's promises to Israel in his word have failed. In answer he observes that even in the Old Testament not all who were Jews by blood could be counted as true members of Israel (9:6ff.). Even among the children of Abraham a stark division existed between the 'children of the promise' and those who were outside his election promises. So Paul implies that God's word and promises are still fulfilled in those who respond to God's electing call to faith in Jesus as Messiah. Jesus' disciples follow in the direct line of succession from the faithful believers in the Old Testament who formed the true Israel. So the promises of God remain effective.

Is God unjust in his judgment? (9:14–33)

Again the heckler interposes: 'If God's election determines who will be accepted as true Israel and who will be rejected, is God unjust to condemn those whose position and sin was ultimately determined by God himself?' Paul strongly resists any such questioning of God's sovereign right to chose or to reject whoever he wants. Like a potter, God has the absolute right over us all to do whatever he wants with us. Paul's argument here seems to resemble the Muslim emphasis on the absolute power of the God who is *akbar*/'great'. But we have to remember that the biblical God is not unfeelingly above his creation without love or personal relationship with his people. So God waits longingly with constant patience for our repentance.

Paul's emphasis on the sovereignty of God and his election is softened too by the fact that we have the responsibility ourselves to 'pursue righteousness' in the right God-appointed way. Israel tried to find righteousness by following the Law/Torah, but her people could never totally succeed in keeping the Law. In contrast to this Jewish failure the Gentiles found righteousness through faith in Jesus the Christ, although they did not have the conscious aim of striving after righteousness (9:30–3). What a paradox! By faith they found what they were not really looking for, while the majority of Israel never found what they desperately searched for. Righteousness comes through faith in Jesus and is therefore readily available to all people and all peoples. Works of Law/Torah are restricted to Jews only, and even they can never attain to full obedience to all the Law.

What about the Law? (10:1–21)
Again, Paul starts this section by reaffirming his longing for Israel's salvation. He is no ivory-tower theologian who can speak of God's purposes and human salvation or damnation with cool detachment. Like God himself, Paul is passionately involved in the emotional reality of what he is saying. True biblical theology will always relate both rationally and emotionally to living mission situations.

Paul shows once more his positive attitude to his own people. He notes approvingly that they are zealous in their pursuit of righteousness – is this not a challenge and rebuke to many of us as Christians? But zeal for God does not suffice. Zeal can be misplaced and unenlightened. How often this truth is seen in the practice of the various faiths – Hindus climbing hundreds of stone steps on their knees, Hinayana Buddhists meditating for long hours without eating or sleeping, Muslims fasting without food or water through the heat of the day. Israel's zeal, Paul notes, sought to establish their own righteousness by their good works and their own efforts. They were ignorant of the righteousness freely provided for them by God himself through Jesus Christ.

These words lead to the highly significant declaration in 10:4 that 'Christ is the end [*telos*] of the law'. Much ink has been spilled in trying to expound these words. Although God's Law is of course something good and unchangeably valid, it cannot in itself bring justification or salvation. It is merely a ladder to bring us to the Messiah. Its whole purpose is to show us our sin and thus lead us to Jesus, who is the climax, goal and fulfilment of the Law. So in this verse Paul states that the Law's climactic goal is that Christ may lead his believing people into righteousness. Paul demonstrates a very positive attitude to the Law and shows that it has an abiding purpose in bringing people to faith in Christ and thus to righteousness, but at the same time he is denying the typical Jewish boasting in the Law as God's inalienable means of salvation for Israel.

In 10:5 Paul contrasts righteousness based on the Law with that which comes by faith. Following the Law requires considerable striving and searching, but the word of faith is 'near' us (10:8). We don't need to ascend into heaven in a desperate attempt to bring Christ down from his heights there. Nor do we need to descend into the deep to raise Jesus up from the depths. He is already close to us and readily available to those who have faith in him. But that inward faith in our hearts needs to be expressed verbally on our lips (10:9). This truth needs to be repeated in our time, too. Christian faith is no mere private matter. The faith in our hearts needs to be expressed publicly in words. This inevitably raises serious questions about the validity of being a secret believer, as is common in situations of extreme persecution (e.g. many Muslim countries). So Paul declares that justification and salvation come through faith in our hearts which is spoken out in public (10:10). He observes that this is equally true for Jews and Gentiles. God pours out his riches equally on all who call on the name of the Lord without shame.

It may be noted that this confession of the Lord is related to our baptism, for it is summarised in the traditional baptismal confession that 'Jesus is Lord' (10:9). Again we note that the witness of our faith requires public and visible signs. We noticed that in their Christian testimonies, Muslim converts in Singapore consistently emphasised their decision to be baptised, for it was baptism rather than inward faith which brought fierce persecution.

Paul now proceeds to the well-known mission passage in 10:14–17. He is very logical here. While it is true that salvation comes as we call on the name of the Lord, no one can call on Jesus unless they have first believed. But faith requires that we first hear the good news of Jesus. And that means that people must first be called to preach the gospel, so that others may hear and believe. So Paul underlines the primary calling of preaching the good news of Jesus Christ. In our day it is easy to replace that essential calling with all sorts of other mission emphases – development work, ecology, justice, lifestyle, gender issues, peace and reconciliation, prophecy and the state of Israel, etc. While all these may have a place within the message of the gospel, the essential nature of preaching faith in Jesus Christ must remain central.

Having rejoiced in the glories of 10:1–17, Paul sadly comes back to the harsh facts of reality. The gospel has been preached to Israel. They have heard. But they nevertheless remain a 'disobedient and obstinate people' (10:18–21). So Paul has still not found the answer to his questions. God's mission statement still remains under wraps.

God's faithful remnant (11:1–10)

The contrast of 'his people' with the strongly negative 'reject' (11:1) reminds Paul's readers of his strong emotional attachment to Israel and his agony at their failure to enter into the grace of God through Jesus the Messiah. Israel remains 'his people' and the very word 'people'/*laos* implies that close covenant relation-ship between God and his chosen people. But it is this same 'people' who seem now to be rejected by God. Paul asks whether the God of grace and faithful love could ever cast out his people and break his covenant with them.

In facing this terrible question Paul remembers that he himself is an Israelite of the seed of Abraham and from God's specially beloved tribe of Benjamin. So at least one person in the nation of Israel is living in the grace of the Lord! This allows Paul to state categorically that God has not rejected his people. He refers to the Old Testament concept that God always has a remnant among his people who remain faithful. Elijah too had thought that he was the only person in Israel not to bow the knee to false gods and idols but to worship the Lord alone. Elijah had felt his fearful vulnerability as the only true believer when people were trying to kill him. And if they succeeded, he reasoned, then there would not be any believers! But God had reassured him that actually there remained seven thousand faithful believers. There was indeed a remnant. And Paul reassures himself with the words, 'so too at the present time there is a remnant chosen by grace' (11:5). And he contrasts this minority who are chosen by grace, as against the great majority who are 'hardened' and 'cannot see' as they trip over the 'stumbling-block'/*skandalon* (cf. 9:32, 33; 14:13, 21) of Jesus Christ.

Many years ago a young man in an institution for young offenders became a committed believer in Jesus Christ. He was terribly persecuted by the other inmates, who frequently beat him up. He felt utterly alone in his faith. Then one day he went to a large missionary meeting in Bristol. Sitting in the gallery he watched the crowds of Christians gathering. 'Are all these people my brothers and sisters?' he asked. Before the meeting itself even began he was in floods of tears. He had not realised how many Christians there were in Britain. He was not alone in following the Lord. God has not rejected his people. There is a remnant.

And yet Paul remains deeply conscious that it is just a tiny remnant and this can hardly satisfy his longing for the salvation of the multitudes of his people. Is there no hope for them? Has God finally given up on his plans for the salvation of Israel? Has his covenant with Israel been invalidated by their sin and rejection of Jesus?

In this question we stand in a paradox. On the one hand it is true that covenants include the condition of righteous obedience. Sin therefore breaks a covenant. So Israel has no right to claim before God that he should keep his covenant. On the other hand, God remains amazingly gracious and faithful to his word despite our sin. Grace prevails. If this were not true, the new covenant in the blood of Jesus would also mean nothing. The Church has not been without sin in its history. And each one of us as believers has to confess that we have broken his covenant by our sin and unbelief. But grace . . .

So is God's grace still applicable to Israel as a people? What are God's purposes for them?

God's mission statement (11:11–36)
With Paul's passionate concern for his own people Israel, he was inevitably not going to be satisfied with the idea of only a remnant being saved. The concept of a remnant might be adequate theologically to prove that God has not totally rejected his people, but emotionally it is quite insufficient. Paul could not be content that just one or two Jews here and there might accept the grace of God in Jesus Christ. He was concerned for the multitudes of his people. He is longing for the 'fullness'/*pleroma* (11:12) and 'the whole batch' (11:16) of 'all Israel' (11:26) to be saved, as indeed also the 'fullness'/*pleroma* of the Gentiles (11:25, my literal translation). How can this come to pass?

In answering the question as to whether the Jews had stumbled so totally that recovery had become impossible, Paul digs deep into his own mission experience. In Antioch of Pisidia (Acts 13:42–52) the local Jews had been so jealous and embittered when large crowds of Gentiles had accepted the message of Paul and Barnabas they caused severe persecution and social turmoil. Because of the Jews' rejection of the good news of Jesus Christ the apostles had declared: 'We now turn to the Gentiles', and had quoted from the Hebrew Scriptures in Isaiah to support this crucial decision (13:46, 47).

So Paul discovers this mission principle that through the Jews' sin salvation has come to the Gentiles. But he adds that the wonderful glory of salvation in Christ experienced by the Gentiles will in turn make the Jews jealous. I remember an Orthodox Jew once saying bitterly to me, 'The Gentiles have stolen our Jesus and made him into a Gentile'! I quickly reassured him that as a Jew he was very welcome to have Jesus back! Paul foresaw that Jews would become jealous of the Gentiles in their enjoyment of the glories of eternal life in Jesus Christ. Likewise, he says that he rejoices in his own calling as apostle to the Gentiles because in that way he would provoke his fellow Jews to jealousy and thus bring salvation to them also (11:13, 14).

Sadly, it has to be confessed that Paul's vision has generally not worked out. The history of Gentile Christian persecution of the Jews has made most Jews think of Christians as their enemy. They have been provoked more to bitter anger than to jealousy. The Christian Church needs to repent and ask the Holy Spirit to fill us with renewed love. Only with such love in our hearts do we dare to evangelise our Jewish neighbours.

But we must never forget that Paul is still teaching the priority of Jewish evangelism. In our relationships with Israel and the Jewish people we must not be sidetracked from this priority. The Jews' greatest need is for Jesus – not merely for our friendship, nor for assistance in migrating to Israel.

So Paul's vision is that Israel's sin in rejecting Jesus leads to salvation for Gentiles. Then the Gentiles' experience of abundant life will provoke Jews to jealousy and thus bring salvation to some of them. Now he goes further. If the Jews' sin leads to blessing among the Gentiles, how much more will their acceptance bring even greater blessing to the world! Indeed, already at this stage of his argument and in this context he foresees the Jews' 'fullness' – we shall look more closely at this word when expounding 11:25.

Paul has a wonderfully positive view of God's mission purpose.

This is no vicious circle, but rather a blessed spiral: Israel's sin –
Gentile salvation – Jewish jealousy and salvation of some Jews –
yet more blessing to Gentiles – the full inclusion of Jews into
the grace of the Lord. In 11:25, 26, the full inclusion of the Jews
will in turn lead to the ingathering of the fullness of the Gentiles
and all Israel being saved. Small beginnings have large consequences (11:16).

The olive tree (11:17–24)

In the Old Testament God calls Israel an olive tree (Jer. 11:16)
and she is pictured as such. Now Paul develops this imagery as
he engages with God's purposes for the nations. Negative critics
despise Paul's picture as ridiculous – for example, dead branches
which have been cut off from the tree cannot suddenly be grafted
back in! But actually Paul's vivid pictorial teaching speaks clearly.

Because of their unbelief many natural branches will be
lopped off the tree and unnatural ones will be added. Many of
the covenant people of Israel will be rejected, while many
Gentiles will be added to the tree of God's people. And then the
natural Jewish branches will be grafted back into their own tree.
So Paul reminds Gentile believers that they should beware of
pride, for they too could be cut off from the tree of life if they
follow in the unbelieving footsteps of their Jewish neighbour. If
natural branches can be cut off, how much more easily may
unnatural branches be rejected!

It is significant that Paul does not talk of the whole tree being
cut down and replaced by another tree. The old tree of Israel
remains, but now it has Gentile branches added to its Jewish
ones. It is now, therefore, an international community. Some
Gentile Christians have glibly coined the slogan: 'Pentecost is
the birthday of the Church.' This passage totally rejects such an
idea. The very word *ekklesia*/'church' is used in the Septuagint,
the Greek translation of the Old Testament, for the 'congregation'
of Israel (in Hebrew *edah* and *qahal*). The foundation and roots
of the Church lie in Old Testament Israel, the chosen people of
God. And the true Israel of faith has now developed into the

international Church of Jesus Christ with its Jewish roots, but with Gentiles added too.

The crux verses (11:25–32)

Paul now summarises the 'mystery' of God's ultimate mission purpose. Some of Israel has been hardened in unbelief (11:25) until the fullness of the Gentiles has come in. 'And so all Israel will be saved' (11:26). Controversy rages concerning the meaning of the words 'fullness' (NIV interpretation 'full number') of the Gentiles and 'all' Israel. Likewise the word 'so' in verse 26 needs accurate understanding.

Interestingly, Paul had just used the word 'fullness'/*pleroma* with reference to the Jews in 11:12. 'Fullness'/*pleroma* in 11:25 would not seem to imply every individual, but rather people of all nations and backgrounds. So also, when referring to Israel it presumably implies Jews of every type, Sephardic and Ashkenazic, black Ethiopian Jews, Asian Jews from China or India, white European Jews. With the Gentiles, too, Christians may look forward to a multitude of people from every nation and people coming to faith in Jesus Christ. There would seem to be a clear parallel with the vision of Habakkuk that 'the earth will be *filled* with the knowledge of the glory of the LORD' (Hab. 2:14) and Revelation's glorious vision of 'a great multitude which no one could number, from every nation, from all tribes and peoples and tongues, standing before the throne' (Rev. 7:9, NRSV).

There would seem to be a clear parallelism between 'fullness' and 'all'. Just as 'fullness' signifies multitudes of Gentiles from every background but not every individual, so also 'all' refers to Jews of every type. But neither deny the tragic reality of judgment for those who reject Jesus and in unbelief refuse his salvation. Yet while we reject the universalism which believes in the ultimate salvation of every person, these verses do seem to look forward to a glorious future in which we shall witness whole crowds of Jews and Gentiles coming into faith and eternal life in Jesus Christ. What a wonderful prospect! This is the ultimate and assured goal of our mission. Not just one or two believers here and there. We can anticipate huge mass movements of both Jews and Gentiles of every people pressing into the Church of Jesus Christ. In every country, among every people, crowds will believe in Jesus Christ.

The word 'so'/*houto* designates the manner in which something happens, not the timing of the event. Paul is not particularly saying that the ingathering of the fullness of the Gentiles must precede the salvation of all Israel. He is declaring that the salvation of Gentiles is the means by which the Jews will come to faith in Jesus. This clearly parallels 11:11–14.

A few strongly Reformed commentators have interpreted 'all Israel' as meaning all the elect of every nation who have been chosen by God for salvation. The context, however, clearly denies that interpretation. In the preceding part of the chapter, Paul is obviously talking about the Jewish people when he uses the word 'Israel'. And immediately after 11:25–6 he quotes the prophets that it is from Zion or Jacob that ungodliness is removed. It is his covenant with Israel which declares the washing away of all their sins.

Glory!

So Paul summarises this mission statement with the superb prospect of 11:28–32. Here at last he sees God's positive vision for Israel. They may at present be rejecting God's grace in Jesus Christ and thus be enemies of the gospel now, but they are still God's beloved and chosen people because of God's covenant with previous generations of their ancestry. God's gracious gifts and his call are irrevocable (11:29). The key words are 'disobedience' and 'mercy'. Not only has Israel fallen into the sin of disobedience, but the Gentiles are equally under sin. But human disobedience gives way to the universal mercies of the God of all grace. The glorious summary thrills us all: 'God has bound all people over to disobedience so that he may have mercy upon them all'(11:32). God's gracious mercy in Jesus Christ will flow to the multitudes of every nation, Jew and Gentile. No wonder the chapter concludes with the doxology, praising

God with the prayerful purpose that 'to him be the glory for ever!'

Chapters 12 to 15: 'Therefore I urge you . . .'

In chapter 12, verses 1 and 2, heartfelt emotion mixes with solid reason and down-to-earth pragmatism. This combination is vital for the Christian life and for mission.

Paul does not merely suggest that the Roman Christians consider the possibility of offering their bodies as living sacrifices – if convenient, and if it would not overstep their comfort zone! He 'urges' (RSV 'appeal', KJV 'beseech'). Paul is not afraid to express his strongly felt emotions, for the call of the gospel is urgent and allows no coolly uninvolved detachment.

But Paul's emotions go together with solid theological reasoning. His appeal to the Romans is founded on the whole argument of chapters 1 to 11 and so begins with 'therefore' (12:1). It is also firmly and specifically connected with his previous statement (11:32) concerning the mercies of God for people of all nations: 'in view of God's mercy'. And the offering of their bodies is inseparably linked to the renewing of their minds (12:2).

Paul's pragmatism is shown by his down-to-earth emphasis on the Romans' bodies. Later manuscripts have added 'and spirits', as also in 1 Corinthians 6:20. Some Christians are happy to offer their spirits to the Lord with loud hallelujahs and fervent prayer, but Paul requires the presentation of our bodies. It is in our bodies that we are called to glorify God (1 Cor. 6:20). In my experience, believers' spirits will happily and quickly follow their bodies – but sometimes our bodies are rather slow to follow our spirits! Paul is very practical. It is our bodies God demands – and our spirits can follow later!

Paul is obviously relating the offering of our bodies to the Old Testament sacrifices, in which sacrificial animals were dedicated to the Lord. When once they had been presented to God, they no longer belonged to their original owners. Likewise we offer our bodies in a once-for-all sacrifice and then become totally the property of the Lord. The animals presented had to be spotless and perfect. So also we are to be holy and God-like in goodness. It is this self-offering which Paul sees as true worship. In modern times Christians have concentrated considerably on worship – and differing forms of worship have been the cause of considerable heated debate and even church splits. Paul emphasises sacrificial service of God as the life of true worship. And he adds to worship the interesting adjective translated as 'spiritual', but actually it is *logiken*, which means 'of the word'. Our worship is to be biblical in accordance with God's word and it is to bear the stamp of the nature of Christ as God's incarnate Word.

Only through offering our bodies with renewed minds for Christ's service can we experience the will of God in our lives – and how encouraging that his will is not only good and acceptable, but absolutely perfect (12:2). There is nothing better than living sacrificially for Christ – such a life is perfect!

In this life of service Christians should use their minds to think humbly and not exalt themselves. Paul relates this particularly to the use of spiritual gifts. We are united as the one body of Christ, but each person within the body has different gifts. Nobody has all the gifts and no one gift is given to all. We may note that the list of gifts in 12:4–8 differs almost totally from the list in Corinthians. Such lists are merely a random selection of God's gifts to us. They are not exhaustive. The NIV has one misleading mistranslation: the word 'govern' is not in the original Greek and gives a wrong idea of leadership carrying power and authority. Jesus, however, clearly taught that Christian leaders should not exercise authority (Mark 10:42, 43). Human leaders are mere under-shepherds, while God and his biblical word carry the authority.

But let us use the gifts the Holy Spirit gives us in loving humility for the welfare of the Church and for the glory of the Lord! It is in this context that Paul underlines the central importance of love (12:9) and shows a variety of ways in which love must be worked out (12:9–21).

Governments

In the Christian life God demands that wives 'submit'/*hupotasso* to their husbands (1 Pet. 3:1, 5), that Christians submit to all who are dedicated to the Lord's service (1 Cor. 16:16), that younger people submit to their elders (1 Pet. 5:5), servants to their masters (1 Pet. 2:18), all of us to Christ (Eph. 5:24), and indeed we are all to submit in humility to one another (Eph. 5:21). Using the same word, Paul now declares that Christians are to submit to 'governing authorities' (13:1, 5).

As Delling says in *The Theological Dictionary of the New Testament* (Gerhard Kittel *et al.*, Wm. B. Eerdmans Publishing Company), the word used for 'submit' 'does not mean so much "to obey", but rather in relationship to other people "to lose or surrender one's own rights or will" '. No one has the right to demand that another person 'submit' to them, and it does not imply an unthinking attitude of obedience. But it does mean that you place yourself alongside and below the other. With governments, too, it does not mean that one must always be obedient and subservient, but together with the governing authorities one submits to them in their task of commending those who do good and judging those who do wrong.

It is well to remember that Paul is writing this letter at a time when the Roman authorities were severely persecuting Christians. The context is therefore not of a benign democratic state, but of a cruel anti-Christian autocracy. Submission to any human authority is always subject to our overriding submission to God and his commands. But in so far as the government is fulfilling its task of supporting the good and opposing evil, the Christian is called supportively to submit.

In this, as in all our behaviour, the Christian should be acutely aware that the final day of full salvation is drawing near and 'the day is almost here' (13:12). We are therefore to 'put on the armour of light' and 'clothe [ourselves] with the Lord Jesus Christ'.

Dedication to Christ and to his mission service in taking his mercies to the world must replace all gratification of 'the desires of the sinful flesh' (13:14). We remember the Lord's own words, 'not my will, but yours be done' (Luke 22:42), and the words of the Lord's Prayer, 'thy will be done'.

The weak and the strong (chapters 14 and 15)

As we noted earlier, the Roman church seems to have been divided into various house churches. Some of them consisted of Gentile believers, while others had Jewish Christians. Each had different traditions and found it hard to accept the validity of the other's preconceived ideas. The Jewish believers still held tight to the traditions of Jewish Law with only kosher food and careful observation of the Sabbath. On the other hand, the Gentile Christians gloried in their freedom from such legalism and claimed that they were not under the Law. Both tended to judge each other and real fellowship was lacking.

There was also apparently some division with regard to eating meat which had been offered at pagan shrines – a practice which was not only fundamental in the guilds of that time but also exists today in non-Christian Chinese and many other societies. Some scrupulous Christians therefore refused all meat in order to be on the safe side.

Christians today can readily understand these situations of disagreement. The generation gap is often strong and divisive in the Church. Charismatic Christians and more traditional Reformed believers may not find it easy to worship together and enjoy true fellowship. Christians of different ethnic backgrounds may also judge one another. Jewish Christians may react against Gentile churches – and vice versa. At All Nations Christian College we have sometimes experienced problems with modern British students who drink alcohol and emphasise freedom in the Spirit while some African or Asian students abhor the very idea of alcohol, the cinema, etc.

Paul tends to align himself with 'the strong', those who are free from the Law. And he exhorts the strong to 'bear with the failings of the weak'(15:1). But all of us should aim to please the other, not to please ourselves. Our desire is to 'build up' the other, not shatter their faith. So we strive after a 'spirit of unity' as we follow Christ. We want to glorify God with one heart and with one united mouth (15:6).

The key command in this passage is that we 'accept one another, then, just as Christ accepted you' (15:7). Jesus is so mercifully gracious in accepting all of us with all our weaknesses and foibles, so let us follow him in accepting our brothers and sisters with their varying backgrounds and attitudes. Again, we note that the final goal, even in these very down-to-earth matters of relationships, is that not only Jews may glorify the Lord, but also the Gentiles of every nation and people (15:8-12). That is the context of our being filled with joy, peace and hope by the power of the Holy Spirit – indeed, we are not only so filled by the Holy Spirit, but we overflow with a living hope that reaches out to Jews and Gentiles in all the world (15:13).

As noted earlier, Paul goes on in the second half of chapter 15 to testify to his own ministry as apostle to the Gentiles. He has become like a sacrificial priest preaching the good news of Jesus Christ to the Gentiles that they might become an offering to God which is sanctified by the Holy Spirit. His work is to preach the good news to the Gentiles; the Holy Spirit will then make them pure and holy – the Spirit is indeed the Spirit of holiness.

Paul proceeds to recount something of the evangelistic church-planting ministry he has already had and looks forward to the future. He must go to Jerusalem with the Gentile churches' gift, then visit the church in Rome and move on to further mission to Spain. In this he declares that he does not want to build on other workers' foundations, but feels called to pioneer evangelism. As we have observed already, modern mission in our century desperately needs both pioneer workers like Paul and also those who will minister in, under and through existing churches.

Final greetings (chapter 16)

This final chapter, with its long list of greetings, shows how strongly Paul believed in good personal relationships. Most of the people greeted will have been known personally to Paul, but probably there were also some he had never met. Nevertheless, their names were known to him as leaders in the Roman church, brothers and sisters who were living and working with the same goals as Paul. Paul had never been in Rome and he had no automatic authority there because he had not himself planted the church in Rome. Now, in preparation for his coming to Rome and then on to Spain, he wanted to establish a close link with the leading Christians in Rome.

Beware those who bring division!

Romans 16 is unique among Paul's letters in including a stark warning against false teachers in the midst of his final greetings (16:17–20). This has caused some commentators to query whether these verses have been misplaced or even whether they are genuinely part of this epistle. But there is strong textual evidence to support these verses being part of Paul's original letter and being located just where we find them in chapter 16. They also fit the context. In chapters 14 and 15, Paul has been dealing with potential and perhaps actual divisions in the church in Rome. Jewish and Gentile house churches were not in harmony together. Now, even in his final greetings, he again warns against 'those who cause divisions'. Once again we observe how vitally important loving unity is among Christians. 'Smooth talk and flattery' easily deceive Christians who are naïve and not solidly grounded in biblical teaching (16:18). And Paul observes that those who sow dissension and division among Christians are often 'serving . . . their own appetites', bolstering their own positions of leadership and power among God's people. Paul unhesitatingly and boldly declares that such people are 'not serving our Lord Christ' although they may sound highly spiritual and teach with dynamic. Such people have afflicted and still afflict the Church throughout history and in all parts of the world.

Paul assumes that Christians should stick firmly to the traditional apostolic teaching which they had received. Immature ears itch for what is new and have weak biblical and theological roots. Culturally the western world urges us towards what is new and is bored with what is old and traditional. In Islam, and likewise in Confucian-influenced cultures, the old is true and good while the new and innovative is by definition heretical and false. As Christians we stand firmly on our traditional biblical and theological roots, but also strive forward towards the glorious hope which awaits us. Culturally, too, we not only maintain the old roots, but also fly with contemporary, relevant wings. The foundational apostolic teaching needs to be applied to modern situations and society.

Freed slaves

It is often pointed out that the different classes of people in Roman society tended to have names that reflected their status. This allows us to see what sort of people Paul is greeting in this chapter. From this we may also deduce something of the character of the church in Rome. As various commentators have shown, it would seem that most of the names listed here indicate that they were freed slaves. But there were also among the Roman Christians several who were sufficiently wealthy to have house churches meeting in their homes. This would indicate some degree of wealth. In verse 23, Erastus evidently held a high position in Roman society, so must also have been a man of some means. But we also know from Paul's letter to Philemon that actual slaves were becoming Christians too and it is probable that the church in Rome included such slaves. Although the church in Rome consisted largely of freed slaves, it did not therefore exclude people of other backgrounds. Rich and poor, Jew and Gentile, free and slave joined together through faith in Jesus Christ. This radical practice of social equality in the Church proved a time-bomb which would finally eliminate slavery itself.

In a society which was riven by class and ethnic distinctions the challenge to Christian unity was daunting. But the reality of such loving oneness in Christ presented the Roman empire with an ideal which the world could not match. Was this one reason why the Church grew so rapidly in those days?

In modern times, too, the Church faces the same challenges. Just as the Roman church was apparently divided into separate Jewish and Gentile home groups, so in our time too we frequently observe churches which are divided along ethnic lines. In years past the Church Growth Movement pointed out that homogeneous groups grow better than mixed churches, because in this way people only face the stumbling-block of the gospel rather than being presented with cultural barriers. And I know for myself how much I enjoy a Jewish Christian gathering from time to time, which allows for Jewish humour, Jewish communication, worship and biblical teaching which is relevant to us as Jews. But homogeneous fellowships also need wider fellowship with Christians of other ethnic backgrounds, for their own welfare as well as for the sake of our witness in a society riven with racial prejudice.

Likewise, the Church today needs to break down the barriers presented to us by the generation gap. Churches which are purely old people or youth will inevitably be lopsided in their Christian life and inadequate in their wider witness.

The church in Rome was, as we have noted, largely consisting of freed slaves. These would generally be people of middle status. In the western world, too, the Church has traditionally mainly attracted the middle class, while in some other countries it has particularly drawn people of higher education. In past years in some Latin American countries the Church particularly attracted the poor and uneducated, but over the years this has changed. With their Christian faith, Latin American Christians have prospered, with better education and economic development. Inevitably Christians stop wasting their money on excessive drinking, smoking and gambling. With new faith in God's word they begin to read more, and as part of the wider Church they gain knowledge of the whole world. They also become honest and reliable workers, so economic prospects open up. Some years ago, in Chile, I was shocked to see notices outside businesses and factories advertising job vacancies with the words 'Pentecostals preferred'! This was no religious discrimination, but a recognition that Christians make better workers – this has been true sometimes in post-Communist Russia also. So poorer Christians may gradually be drawn socially into the middle classes.

But the Roman church never allowed itself to remain restricted to the one type of person. And Paul is strongly urging them to accept each other and relate lovingly together. Yet at the same time he does not ask the Jewish and Gentile house churches actually to merge. What a model for Christians everywhere! We need to maintain the balance between homogeneous groupings and wider fellowship.

Women

Paul is sometimes accused of being negative about women, but this chapter gives the lie to such calumnies. It is remarkable in this chapter how Paul exalts and gives honour to so many women in his greetings. Nobody could accuse him of chauvinism in this chapter! What a list of women – Phoebe, Prisca, Mary, Junias, Tryphaena, Tryphosa, Persis, Rufus' mother, Julia, Nereus' sister (RSV spellings).

It would seem that several of these women were wealthy, with homes of sufficient size to host a house church: for example, Prisca (4). It is noteworthy that her name is mentioned before that of her husband Aquila, for she was the leader in the church in their home. And Phoebe too seems to have hosted a church in her home in Cenchreae, the port of the city of Corinth.

Paul adds significant descriptions to the names of these Christian women. Phoebe was a deaconess, following on from the appointment of this serving ministry in Acts 6. In 1 Timothy 3:11 Paul gives further instructions concerning the character which should be the precondition before a woman is authorised to be a deacon. It is interesting that in 1 Timothy 3 it is the men deacons (not particularly the women deacons) who are to be marked out in society as having well-ordered households and disciplined children.

Prisca and her husband are honoured with the observation that they were Paul's fellow-workers in Christ Jesus, ones who were willing even to risk death for the sake of the spread of the gospel among the Gentiles. The title 'fellow-workers' implies such a relationship with Paul which is almost an embryonic mission society (cf. Phil. 2:18, 25). Mary too was one who worked hard among Christians in the Church – how often throughout history it has been women who have done the bulk of the work in their church! Junia was not only spiritually closely related to Paul and shared with him the honour of having been in prison for the gospel, but she was a believer in Jesus before Paul was converted. Together with Andronicus she was evidently well known in the Church of Jesus Christ. And both of them were 'apostles', the most significant ministry and title in the first-century Church. The word 'apostle' carries with it considerable leadership responsibility.

Although readers of Romans cannot avoid the challenging fact that in the Roman church women were accepted both as deacons and as apostles, perhaps the central reality is that they were 'saints' (15). As sisters and brothers in Christ who are equally set apart as godly ministers of the good news of Jesus Christ, we all share together without distinction of status as children of the Father and as witnesses to the gospel.

The final blessing (16:25–7)
Paul concludes his personal greetings by prayerfully commending the Christians at Rome to God. It is God who is able to strengthen the Christians for their life of witness in Rome. The Greek word used for 'establish' means that the Christians will be so supported by God that they will be firm and steadfast, upright and unshakeably immovable. In all the vicissitudes and pressures of life nothing will be able to shake their faith. No persecution or discrimination will be able to move them. Sneers and mockery

will never undermine the assured certainty of their witness. Paul's prayer for the Christians in Rome is exactly what we need today.

Such assured and unswerving faith can only be produced through the good news of Jesus Christ which Paul proclaimed and taught. Paul dares to call this 'my gospel' – he was confident that what he preached was the true gospel of Jesus Christ. Such confidence may today be criticised as 'fundamentalism' or arrogance, but in humility the Christian is called also to a firm assurance of faith. It is by the preached message of Jesus Christ that Christians are made strong. As soon as we stress other things beside the person, relationships and work of Jesus we shall experience weakness and instability among Christians. Everything else, however biblical or Spirit-centred, remains secondary to the centrality of Jesus himself. It is in and through Jesus Christ that we can be rooted and grounded in the Father who strengthens and establishes his people.

In these final verses Paul harks back to his introduction to the whole letter (1:5). His great longing is that Gentiles of all nations might be brought to 'believe and obey'. What was a 'mystery' in Old Testament times has now been revealed through the Scriptures – the God of Israel and the Messiah Jesus are now reaching out to all nations. In this letter Paul has given superb teaching concerning many aspects of Christian discipleship and the life of the Church. Deep theological truths have also been expounded in some detail. But behind and above everything else Paul longs for the preaching of the gospel of Jesus Christ among all nations everywhere. This in turn will lead to such faith that people will live in obedience to God the Father. Thus the holy will of God will be done on earth. What a vision! May the Holy Spirit plant this great purpose in the hearts and minds of us all today!

But even above the missionary vision for the spread of the gospel among all peoples everywhere lies the ultimate purpose both of Paul and of all true believers. We live, work and witness in order that God himself might be glorified through Jesus Christ (16:27). The context of this concluding verse remains, however, the proclamation of the good news of Jesus Christ among all nations. Through this missionary witness God will be praised, worshipped, glorified and served by multitudes of people from every nation throughout the world. Paul and all true Christians long for this great reality, that through the Son and by the Holy Spirit the Father might be given all the glory and honour he deserves. To this end we live and work, preach and teach. To God be the glory!

8

Conclusion: 2,000 years from the New Testament to today

Our study of selected New Testament writers has shown the struggle of Jesus and the first apostles to widen the Church's horizons. No longer were the people of God restricted in their vision merely to the people of Israel. The Church was discovering that the God of Israel has always been the God of all the earth. The long-awaited Jewish Messiah confined his basic ministry to the Jews, but already indicated both by his teaching and by his actual ministry that the doors were now widening to include the Gentiles of all nations.

Already in the Gospels the mixed-race Samaritans were included in the kingdom of God. Even Gentiles from Galilee entered into relationship with the Messiah, together with representatives of the neighbouring Canaanite peoples, the Romans, Greeks and even, through the Wise Men, the wider Gentile peoples. Then, as we have observed, the book of Acts describes the mission of Paul and his associates around the northern shores of the Mediterranean to both Jews and Gentiles. And in the epistles, as we have observed through our study of Romans, the apostles defend their ministry to Gentiles as well as Jews. Thus the New Testament sets the stage for the expansion of the Christian faith throughout the world among all peoples.

While the New Testament focuses our attention on the spread of the good news in southern Europe, it seems that Peter moved east from Israel to Baghdad and what is now Iraq, Lebanon, Syria and even probably up to the southern Caucasus region. At the same time Mark was bringing the gospel to Egypt and thus to the southern shores of the Mediterranean to the peoples of North Africa. It is very probable that Thomas made use of the relatively new discovery of the prevailing trade winds which opened the way to wider trade between the Middle East and southern India. Strong tradition indicates that he planted the first churches around Cochin which became the great Syrian Orthodox Mar Thoma churches of that area.

Having established a relatively firm foundation in the so-called 'civilised' world around the Mediterranean, the mission of the Church began to extend out into central Europe and even the 'uttermost parts', namely northern Europe. Gradually the European tribes yielded to the message of Christ. In Britain, too, the Cornish Patrick evangelised across in Ireland, and then in their turn the Irish sent missionaries from their missionary and monastic centre in Iona to convert the pagan British. Iona reproduced itself in Lindisfarne, which also became a Celtic centre of monastic and missionary life. Meanwhile the Roman church had sent Augustine to the south of England in 597, and Paulinus went from Canterbury to the Anglo-Saxons in the north. Thus, bit by bit, Britain too became Christian.

The so-called 'Dark Ages' witnessed the amazing expansion of the Church throughout western Europe, while the Nestorian Christians spread eastwards along the silk route as far as China and then even into Japan and Indonesia. In the second half of the ninth century Cyril and Methodius ventured out from Greece to evangelise the pagan Slavs, and the Eastern Orthodox Church expanded dramatically. At first the Eastern

Church was centred on Constantinople/Istanbul. But after this great city fell to the Muslim armies and Russia became safe from the centuries of Mongol ravages, Moscow became known as the 'third Rome'. Later the Russian Orthodox churches took the gospel across the vast steppes of Siberia, eventually reaching Alaska and Japan.

As transport improved, the western world began an era of worldwide discovery and then of colonialism. Coinciding with this wider vision of the world, a concern for international mission developed among Christians. The Franciscans and Dominicans led the way for the Roman Catholic Church, and then the Jesuits pioneered a more contextually relevant form of mission in reaction to the Roman Church's losses under the Reformation. The Roman Church had lost whole tracts of European land to the Protestants, so the Jesuits longed to compensate by subduing new lands in South America, Asia and elsewhere to the rule of the Church. It took time for the new Reformation churches to put their theory of international mission into practice, but gradually this evolved through the Reformed Church of Holland, the Moravians and others. Later, the great William Carey pioneered English-speaking mission to India and thus opened the door for missionaries from Britain to spread the gospel throughout the British Empire and even beyond.

For many centuries Europe remained the centre of the Christian Church – to such an extent that it is still a danger that some people in other continents think of Christianity as a European faith. But intrepid European Christians migrated to America, Australasia, South Africa and many other parts of the world. They carried with them the good news of Jesus Christ, and thus the gospel spread widely. As the European Church became somewhat traditional and tired, it lost much of its vitality. Liberalism and then pluralism undermined the very roots of its message. As the Church declined, the Christian centre of gravity shifted to America, which remains to this day the largest missionary-sending country in the world. And much contemporary mission thinking and mission strategies still stem from America.

But in more recent decades God has moved on once more. His Spirit has brought vital Christian life and a passion for international mission to many of the churches of Asia, Latin America and Africa. South Korea is now the second largest source, after USA, of long-term cross-cultural missionaries. Recently my wife was speaking in a conference for expatriate workers in a North African country and was encouraged to find that 10 per cent of those present came from Latin America. Latin American Christians are now reversing the trends of colonialism and evangelising Spain and Portugal. Tens of thousands of committedly Christian Filipinos are working outside their own country, many of them in Muslim countries which are closed to conventional mission work. God is now mobilising his Church worldwide for mission all over the world.

This task of mission is not only pioneer evangelism and church planting, but many expatriate workers are also involved in the teaching and training of national Christians. It remains God's desire that the Church should become Christ's perfect bride without the warts of unholiness and sin. Particularly in Latin America and black Africa, multitudes of people flock into the churches with a vibrant profession of loving faith in Jesus Christ, but sometimes these Christians are wafer-thin in their faith, with little depth of holiness or of biblical teaching. It is the task of mission today to rectify that weakness in the churches.

In recent decades Christians have become increasingly conscious of the holistic nature of mission. We are called to socio-political involvement to help rectify the tragic circumstances of so many poorer and oppressed people. Missionaries join with Christ in his compassion for the multitudes. Street children, prostitutes and down-trodden women, child labourers, victims of drought or other natural disasters, those suffering from the agonies of war and violence – all such situations touch the heart of our loving Father and move Christians to holistic mission.

The New Testament looks forward not only to renewed men

and women, but also to a new heaven and a new earth. The world was created by Christ and also exists 'for him' (Col. 1:16). It is therefore incumbent on us as Christians to take care of his creation so that we can present it to him in all its beauty and perfection. Ecology is not only for the welfare of humanity, but also for the pleasure and satisfaction of our creator God. It is a significant part of Christian mission.

Every aspect of international mission finds its source and foundation in the New Testament. It is my prayer that readers of this book will allow the New Testament to convey its message of God's passionate worldwide concern for Jews and Gentiles of every nation. May the Holy Spirit use his word to stir up his people to share the good news of Jesus Christ in its fullness to a world which desperately needs him. We believe that in Jesus Christ we have abundant life and salvation, the ultimate answer to every need and heartache.

Suggested reading

General reading

Kaiser, W. C., *Mission in the Old Testament: Israel as a Light to the Nations*, Baker Books, 2000.

Kostenberger, A. J. and O'Brien, P. T., *Salvation to the Ends of the Earth*, IVP, 2001.

Senior, D. and Stuhlmueller, C., *The Biblical Foundations for Mission*, SCM, 1983.

Matthew

Carson, D. A., *The Expositor's Bible Commentary*, vol. 8, Zondervan, 1984.

Davies, M., *Matthew*, JSOT Press, 1993.

France, R. T., *Matthew* (Tyndale NT Commentaries), IVP, 1985.

France, R. T., *Matthew – Evangelist and Teacher*, Paternoster, 1989.

Goldsmith, M. F., *Matthew and Mission – the Gospel through Jewish Eyes*, Paternoster, 2001.

Green, M., *The Message of Matthew* (BST), IVP, 2000.

Hagner, D., *Word Biblical Commentary – Matthew*, Word Books, 1993.

Sim, D. C., *The Gospel of Matthew and Christian Judaism*, T. and T. Clark, 1998.

Weaver, D., *Matthew's Missionary Discourse*, Sheffield Academic Press, 1990.

Luke

Fitzmyer, J. A., *The Gospel According to Luke*, Anchor Bible, Doubleday, 1981.

Gooding, D., *According to Luke*, IVP, 1987.

Green, J. B., *The Gospel of Luke*, NICNT, Eerdmans, 1997.

Marshall, I. H., *Luke – Historian and Theologian*, Paternoster, 1970.

Marshall, I. H., *The Gospel of Luke*, Paternoster, 1978.

Navone, J., *Themes of St Luke*, Gregorian University Press, 1970.

Nolland, J., *Word Biblical Commentary – Luke*, Word Books, 1993.

John

Beasley-Murray, G. R., *Gospel of Life – Theology in the Fourth Gospel*, Hendrickson, 1991.

Beasley-Murray, G. R., *Word Biblical Commentary –John*, Thomas Nelson, 1999.

Brown, R. E., *The Gospel According to John*, Anchor Bible, Geoffrey Chapman, 1966.

Carson, D. A., *Jesus and His Friends*, IVP, 1980.

Carson, D. A., *The Gospel According to John*, IVP, 1991.

Kostenberger, A. J., *Encountering John*, Baker Books, 1999.

Milne, B., *The Message of John* (BST), IVP, 1993.

Motyer, S., *Your Father the Devil?*, Paternoster, 1997.

Smalley, S., *John – Evangelist and Teacher*, Paternoster, 1978.

Stibbe, M. W. G., *John*, Sheffield Academic Press, 1993.

Acts of the Apostles

Dunn, J. D. G., *The Acts of the Apostles*, Epworth Press, 1996.

Gooding, D., *True to the Faith*, Hodder & Stoughton, 1990.

Liefeld, W. L., *Interpreting the Book of Acts*, Baker Books, 1995.

Marshall, I. H. and Petersen, D. (eds), *Witness to the Gospel*, Eerdmans, 1998.

Stott, J. R. W., *The Message of Acts* (BST), IVP, 1990.

Romans

Chae, D. J.-S., *Paul as Apostle to the Gentiles*, Paternoster, 1997.

Dunn, J. D. G., *Romans*, Word Books, 1988.

Fitzmyer, J. A., *Romans*, Anchor Bible, Doubleday, 1993.

Moo, D., *The Epistle to the Romans* (NICNT), Eerdmans, 1996.

Morgan, R., *Romans*, Sheffield Academic Press, 1995.

Stott, J. R. W., *The Message of Romans* (BST), IVP, 1994.